Preview Edition

SOMETHING FOR NOTHING:

Shoplifting Addiction & Recovery

by

Terrence Daryl Shulman,
JD,MSW,ACSW,CAC

"It was so worth my time, energy, and commitment to get treatment from Terrence Shulman. I received a healing, cleansing experience that has empowered me and given me clarity over my stealing and dishonesty. I now have the tools to watch out for my warning signs and how to get past them. It was a life changing event."

- Dave S., 31, Port Huron, Michigan

"C.A.S.A. has helped me in many ways. It has made me feel like I'm not alone in my struggles, that other people have the same feelings and it's easy to share and help others. There should be more C.A.S.A. meetings in other places and the problem should be more recognized."

- Jessica, 18, Southgate, Michigan

"I am going before the Parole Board soon. I want help. I've been in too much trouble because of shoplifting and I can't get help anywhere for my addiction. Your program, from what I've heard, helps people express themselves and find ways that others have used to stop stealing. That's what I need: support, so I can stop. I am a good person who lives a good life other than my shoplifting problems. I really need your help."

-Andre M., Michigan Dept. of Corrections,

Camp Kincheloe

"Mr. Shulman's compassion and non-judgmental ways made it easier for me to feel accepted with my addiction problem."

-Amy G., Michigan

"The C.A.S.A. e-mail support group list has given me a place I can find daily understanding, support and motivation on my recovery journey."

-Julia

"The C.A.S.A. e-mail group has been extremely helpful to me because I am able to be in my own comfortable surroundings when I am talking to other members or simply reading the posts. I have found a wonderful group of people out there who share the same addiction as I do. Together, I feel we can beat this thing and live decent lives."

-Mark M., Niles, Michigan

SOMETHING FOR NOTHING:
Shoplifting Addiction & Recovery

by

Terrence Daryl Shulman, JD,MSW,ACSW,CAC

Copyright © 2004 by Terrence Daryl Shulman

ISBN 0-7414-1779-0

Published by:

519 West Lancaster Avenue
Haverford, PA 19041-1413
Info@buybooksontheweb.com
www.buybooksontheweb.com
Toll-free (877) BUY BOOK
Local Phone (610) 520-2500
Fax (610) 519-0261

Printed in the United States of America

Printed on Recycled Paper

Published October 2003

Dedication

I dedicate this book to the millions of people around this world who suffer from the disease of "Something for Nothing" and their families and friends who are affected as well. May this book serve as a lifeline to recovery. You are not alone. There is hope.

I also dedicate this book to my father, Robert Shulman, who died April 20, 1993 at age 53. Dad, you never realized recovery was possible. I wish you had. Your triumphs and pains inspired me to go further with my life. Something good will come of this.

Table of Contents

PART THREE

Exercises

PART FOUR

Related Topics

Acknowledgments

There are so many people I wish to acknowledge, without whom I probably would not be alive today, much less have finished this book. Please forgive me if I have forgotten any of you who have touched my life.

My beautiful & supportive wife, Tina,
My mother Madeline & my step-Dad Jim,
My brothers Jordy, Sam, and Marty,
My nephew Devan,
All of my relatives for their unconditional love and support,

Steve Campbell, mentor and friend, rest in peace,

Paul Plamondon for his tireless work in helping develop our web site and co-moderating our e-mail support group,

My best buddies who have kept me strong and centered: Lee Anzicek, Tom Lietaert, John Stempien, Brett Koon, Dana L. Piper, Scott McWhinney, Marty Peters, Ben Goryca, Rob Koliner, Kevin Lauderdale, Dick Halloran, Josh Barclay, Tom Reedy, Chuck Pavey, Andrew Miller, Michael Fox & Paul Plamondon,

Dana L. Piper for back cover photograph,

Cathy Dyer, of Mandalas Awakening, for book cover design,

Annabelle McIlnay, my editor,

My Goddess cheerleading squad: Julie Koblin, Laura Hansen-Koon, Andrea MacFarland, Sharon Harris, Bryn Fortune, Shanda Siegmund, Stacy Arsht-Fox, Mona Light, Robin Schwartz, Megan Powers, Cindy Chandler, Mary Metcalf, Vicki Zaft, Carol Klawson, Amy Goldstein, Daya Faith Walden, Christina Pavey & Maureen McDonald,

Jennifer Everland of Everland Design,

Benji and Penelope, the love dogs,

My fellow recovering friends in C.A.S.A. (Detroit), especially David N., Fran S., Marty H., Heidi W., & Sandra & Tom J.,

My fellow recovering friends in C.A.S.A.'s e-mail support group (international),

Secular Organization for Sobriety (S.O.S.), especially, June F., Dale, Jim G., Tim, & Chuck,

Landmark Education Corporation, especially the Self-Expression & Leadership Course,

Stan Dale and the angels of the Human Awareness Institute,

Quodoushka,

The Detroit Area Men's Wisdom Council,

The Tuesday morning men's breakfast club,

The Mankind Project,

My friends, the staff at Personalized Nursing LIGHT House, Inc., (especially Marcia Andersen, Joe Paliwoda, & Don Oesterwind, Jr.)

Bert Whitehead, Carol Johnson & Pam Landy,

Shantia Mayer,

James E. Ryan,

Joanie, Moira, Megan & Sylvie –my early proofreaders,

Dr. Eugene Ebner, PhD,

Dr. John Brownfain, PhD, rest in peace,

Dr. Wil Cupchik,

Peter Berlin,

Dr. Marcus Goldman,

Dorothy Hickey,

Lois L. (Shoplifters Anonymous, Minneapolis, MN),

Leo R. (Shoplifters Anonymous, Manhattan, NY),

Elizabeth Corsale (Shoplifters Recovery Program, San Francisco, CA),

My friends in B.N.I.,

Clean House, Inc., and

The folks at www.infinitypublishing.com.

About the Author:

Terrence Daryl Shulman is a native Detroiter, an attorney, therapist, consultant, and recovering shoplifter. He is the founder, and a facilitator of C.A.S.A. (Cleptomaniacs And Shoplifters Anonymous), a weekly support group started in 1992 in the Detroit area. C.A.S.A. is one of only a handful of such groups in North America and the world.

He founded a shoplifting addiction & recovery web site in 1995, now www.shopliftersanonymous.com, which includes statistics, information, articles, books, an e-mail support group with chat room, and therapeutic alternatives.

Mr. Shulman primarily counsels shoplifting addicts and their family members by phone and in person at his Detroit area office. He's worked extensively as a chemical dependency counselor and was a clinic Director.

Mr. Shulman consults within the retail industry and with companies to explore prevention, reduction and treatment strategies for shoplifting and employee theft.

He has been featured on numerous television programs, notably 48 Hours, Fox Files, Inside Edition, Extra!, The Today Show, The Early Show, Ricki Lake, Queen Latifah, CNN News, Fox Cable News, The Discovery Channel and numerous local news programs.

He has been featured in various magazines and newspaper articles in The New York Times, The Chicago Tribune, The Detroit Free Press, The Detroit News, The Metro Times, Lifetime, Health, Redbook, Cosmopolitan, Good Housekeeping TV Guide, and Hour Magazine.

This is Mr. Shulman's first book.

He lives in Southfield, Michigan with his wife Tina.

He's writing another book on employee theft and progressive approaches to prevent, reduce and treat these problems.

Preface

*Consider these statistics from **Shoplifters Alternative**:*

*1 out of 11 (23 million) people shoplift in America.

*There is no typical profile of a shoplifter. A shoplifter can be anyone.

*Contrary to myth, men and women shoplift equally.

* 25% of shoplifters apprehended are juveniles, 75% are adults. 55% of adults began shoplifting in their teens.

*Shoplifters are caught an average of once out of 48 times. They are turned over to the police 50% of the time.

*The vast majority of shoplifters are "non-professionals" who steal not out of financial need or greed but as a response to social and personal pressures in their life.

*Approximately 73% of non-professional shoplifters don't plan their thefts in advance.

*59% of shoplifters often buy some merchandise and steal other merchandise.

*The excitement generated from "getting away with it" produces a chemical reaction resulting in what shoplifters describe as an incredible "high" feeling. Many shoplifters will tell you that this high is their "true reward," rather than the merchandise itself.

*Drug addicts who become addicted to shoplifting describe shoplifting as equally addicting as drugs.

*86% of kids say they know other kids who shoplift

*57% of adults and 33% of juveniles say that it is hard for them to stop shoplifting, even after getting caught.

*Most non-professional shoplifters don't commit other types of crimes. They'll never steal an ashtray from your house and will return to you a $20 bill you may have dropped.

It's this incredible rush! It's like getting something for nothing!

Statistics reveal that most people who shoplift do so *not* out of economic need or greed but in response to pressures and emotional issues in their lives. *"Something for Nothing"* is a disease that affects millions. Whether this is a particularly American phenomenon begs to be studied but this problem pervades the planet.

We are living in the age of Winona Ryder and Enron. Anger and skepticism toward thievery abound. But this is not a book about Winona or Enron. There is something else going on besides simple greed. People try to get ahead at any cost. People feel it's never enough. It's beyond money. It's beyond dollars and cents. *It's beyond sense.*

It seems we, individually and collectively, feel an increasing emptiness.

The simplistic notion that shoplifting and stealing are merely legal or moral issues is wrong. There appears to be more dishonesty than ever these days; yet, tougher laws, more sophisticated security systems, and endless moralism haven't reduced these offenses. In fact, they're on the rise. Stealing, particularly shoplifting, can and often does become addictive.

I'm aware many feel we've gone overboard in labeling everything an addiction, a disease, an illness over which people have limited power and control. Most people understand and accept alcohol and drug addictions. They acknowledge gambling, sex, eating, or shopping as addictions.

But people doubt anyone shoplifting or stealing may also be crying out for help. Because we have no real understanding or acceptance of this, those who suffer sink farther into shame, ignorance and denial, and get farther from the sparse real help available. The person, the family, businesses, the economy, and society all suffer for it.

Shoplifting is the primary form of theft I will address in this book but I will touch upon others as well. I do not make excuses for stealing, breaking the law, or dishonesty in general. But I do intend to challenge the notion that most shoplifters are "plain thieves."

This is the first book written on this subject by a recovering shoplifter. I may be accused of bias. So be it. During my recovery, I found no literature to help me. I felt alone. I looked for self-help and support groups. There were none. In 1992 I started a self-help group called C.A.S.A., which stands for Cleptomaniacs And Shoplifters Anonymous. I changed the "K" to a "C" to create the acronym "Casa" which means "home" in Spanish. I wanted to create a safe place for people to share and get help. I intended the group's focus to be on shoplifting but did not want to exclude people who had other forms of addictive theft; thus, I included the term kleptomania as an implied catch-all for stealing issues.

This is the first book written on this subject which posits shoplifting as an addiction rather than an impulse control disorder, kleptomania, or a condition which must be treated only with medication, therapy or both. I am taking this subject matter to the heart of mainstream thinking, hopefully making it more accessible and less shameful.

I hope this book will inspire people to form self-help groups throughout the country and the world where shoplifting addicts can receive and, ultimately, give help. Currently there is no national "umbrella" group for shoplifters. I know of groups only in Manhattan, Minneapolis, San Francisco, and here in Detroit. There are court-ordered educational groups in most states which address shoplifting and economic crimes but most take place over several hours and are of limited value, especially to anyone addicted to shoplifting.

Since starting www.shopliftersanonymous.com in 1998, I have received thousands of e-mail messages seeking information and support. Most people ask if there's a group in their town. Time and time again I've had to tell them: "Not yet. Start one like I did." But few have. Why not? This is the cutting edge. Substantial individual and collective ignorance persists about shoplifting as an addictive-compulsive disorder. Those who know they have a problem feel such overwhelming shame they would never think to tell anyone or seek help. The fear and shame of attending a shoplifting support group, much less starting one, is enormous. I've met people who feel too ashamed to tell their own therapists they shoplift. They fear judgment so they stay silent.

It may take another generation before we have shoplifting recovery groups across the country. But it will happen. There is a need which will be met.

Neither my story nor the stories that follow are intended to make excuses for stealing or shoplifting. I'm not suggesting shoplifting addicts go unpunished. Any illegal act, be it illegal gambling, drug offenses, or drunk driving, must have legal consequences. However, our stories illustrate how good but vulnerable people try to cope with life at pivotal times and how punishment is not enough to stop shoplifters. Our stories go more in depth than previous stories in the scant literature available on shoplifting or kleptomania. I hope this will provide clarity and hope for those who have little of either.

My main intent is to create more awareness of and understanding about shoplifting addiction and offer more solutions so people can get the help they need. Not all people cope the same way and addictions have their similarities but also their differences. People who get hooked on shoplifting need specialized treatment.

Thirteen years ago, I started a new life when I decided I wanted to stop shoplifting. There are millions for whom shoplifting remains "a cry for help." I didn't know how much of a problem it was in my life until I woke up. I'm still waking up every day. I got my life back from the brink of suicide and found it is worth living, with all its challenges and uncertainties, its pains and frustrations.

As the second anniversary of 9/11 passed, one may ask: What does a book on shoplifting addiction matter in the grand scheme of things? I hope this book will be part of a larger solution. *There really is no such thing as something for nothing.* I hope you will join me in some way to reshape the world into a more honest, trusting, and healed place. A place where fewer people try to get something for nothing and more give something for nothing. *"With true giving, after having given, we have more, not less. "*

Terry Shulman
Southfield, Michigan
October 2003

*Quote by Peter Rengel from Living Life in Love

Introduction

I believe we develop beliefs throughout our lives which become our truths.

Over the years of exploring my beliefs as well as those of thousands of shoplifters-in person, by e-mail, letter, and phone-I have found a string of commonly held beliefs:

*"Life is unfair."
*"The world is an unsafe place."
*"Nobody will be there to take care of me."
*"Nobody's really honest."
*"I'm entitled to something extra for my suffering."
*"Nice people finish last."
*"There's not going to be enough money to live."
*"It's a 'dog-eat-dog world' out there."
*"No matter how hard I try, things never work out."
*"It's not worth my speaking up about anything."

These beliefs fuel shoplifting and stealing. Most people are unconscious of their thoughts or they may be prone to "stinking thinking." All behavior-whether freely chosen or stemming from an addictive-compulsive mind set-originates from our thoughts, beliefs, and values. Strong feelings bolster this foundation and, eventually, we act out habitually or with hell-bent righteousness.

I know a woman whose father shoplifted. "He used to tell us: 'It's there for the taking.'" What beliefs would you guess are behind that statement? Would it help to know her father was a war veteran who felt less than heroic, was discontent with his own life choices, and felt powerless, passionless, resentful?

How about the well-to-do woman who has been arrested twice for shoplifting dolls in the last year since her child died?

This book is a call to action–not about making excuses! We've lost our compass. We need to look at ourselves in a new way. We point the finger at the world, everybody else. Or we point our finger at ourselves.

"Thou shalt not steal" is more than a commandment. It is a prerequisite to a life that works: for each of us and all of us, individually and collectively.

With most addictions, we focus on dishonesty as a by-product of the addictive lifestyle. Here, we go to the core: we explore dishonesty-in the form of shoplifting and stealing-as the primary manifestation of unresolved issues and erroneous, destructive beliefs.

This book is like no other. Hopefully, there is something here for everybody: shoplifter, family or friend, therapist, judge, probation officer, attorney, police officer, store or business owner, minister, or student of human behavior. I ask you to take your new insights and apply them to make a difference in the world.

This book is divided into three parts:

Part One highlights my story and the stories of a few others who have attended Cleptomaniacs And Shoplifters Anonymous and have gained insight into how they became addicted to shoplifting and how they changed their lives through an ongoing recovery program.

Part Two provides a guide to the common reasons why people begin shoplifting, important data, statistics, and challenges and issues that arise in recovery.

Part Three includes exercises to help people stop shoplifting and to move toward greater peace and wholeness.

Part Four focuses on related topics which did not fit as well in the other parts.

Part One

Stories

<u>my story</u>

I was born on June 27, 1965. Twenty-five years later, I was a shoplifting addict. Halfway through law school, I sat in a jail cell, one arm handcuffed to the wall. With the other I reached into the nearby wastebasket and plucked out a blurred and discarded mug shot of myself to keep as a memento. The expression on my face: lost, captured, pitiful.

My story is similar in ways, unique in others, to the stories of the thousands of shoplifters I've come to know since I started C.A.S.A. in 1992. *My name is Terry and I'm a recovering shoplifter.* I'm also an attorney, addictions counselor, writer, and soul-searcher. Why did I begin shoplifting and how did I become addicted? I realize one person's explanation is another's excuse.

The first six years of my life were normal, though I have few clear memories. My father was a child prodigy pianist who made a name for himself locally and nationally. He became an attorney around the time I was born but taught piano and performed periodically. My mother was a school teacher on hiatus for the home life. When my brother, Jordy, was born-- I was six--I was excited but jealous as he "stole" my attention. I was no longer "the king." My parents were having marital problems. My Dad was alcoholic. I felt anxious a lot and must've looked for ways to comfort myself.

When I had friends come over my house and they wanted to leave but I didn't want them to, I'd do things like stand in front of the door to try to keep them from leaving. *I didn't want to be left alone. I needed some control.* I have a vague recollection of a friend taking a toy from me or taking a toy

1

from a friend. I know I feared something being taken away from me.

I also had a recurring ear infection from the age of three. I couldn't hear well during the formative years of my speech. This led to a speech impediment, a lisp. At times I still have difficulty pronouncing my "s" sounds and my "z." Other kids made fun of me. I was called out of classes to attend speech class. It was embarrassing. *I felt I was different, there was something defective about me.* I felt powerless to change it. I was angry at God: "Why did this happen to me?" My Mom spent a lot of time helping me with it. Fortunately, it improved and didn't stop me in my life.

My parents divorced when I was ten. I felt my family was taken away. I was angry, especially toward my father. But I suppressed it all. I saw my Mom go through a tough time, too. I had no choice except to be strong, grow up. It wasn't safe to be needy--my Mom was needy, my brother was needy, the family was needy. *I was needy but couldn't show it.* Nobody forced this role on me. I took it on. I had to be the man, a surrogate father for my brother, a surrogate husband to my Mom. We were on welfare, food stamps. I was furious at my father for not paying child support regularly. I felt unloved and anxious about money all the time.

the first time I heard the word "shoplifting"

The first time I heard the word "shoplifting," coincidentally, was around this time. My best friend's teenage sister was arrested at a local department store. A police car dropped her off in front of her house. A crowd gathered. My Mom explained to me what happened. I was shocked but intrigued. I remember thinking: "Wow, what guts. Who would think to do that?" Within days of this event, I was at that same store. I saw a bag of gum balls in the candy aisle, already opened. I looked over my shoulders, daringly picked one out. *I felt a sense of danger and fear but it was also a thrill.* I didn't tell anyone. I felt guilty. *But a seed was planted.*

In my early teens, I had several traumatic incidents where things were stolen from me. I grew up in Detroit in a decent neighborhood but it was never completely safe. I got a new bike for my 11th birthday. I didn't have the patience to wait until I bought a lock for it. I rode it to the nearby store. I came out thirty seconds later. It was gone. I was devastated. I was angry at myself, angry at the person who took it, angry at life. *It was a shock to my system.*

A year later, I was into skateboarding. I was a tough kid growing up in Detroit, but still naively trusted people. One day I was outside my house with my friend, Mikie. A strange kid came by on a bike and asked if I had a screwdriver to fix his bike. I left my skateboard on the lawn and went in to get the tool. When I came back out, Mikie was gone, the kid was gone, and my skateboard was gone. He told Mikie he wanted to see how fast he could skateboard to the end of the block. Mikie fell for it and the kid took off with my skateboard. I was horrified, angry at Mikie and myself for being stupid.

The next day, my Mom and I drove around in her car. I spotted the kid on his bike. We made him get in the car and take us back to his house to retrieve my skateboard. He looked embarrassed and concocted some lie that his twin brother had brought home a skateboard that was probably mine. He brought it to me. *I experienced a sense of satisfaction, a feeling of getting something back that was take from me.*

My satisfaction, however, was short-lived. Later that Summer, I was in front of my house with a few friends. An old car pulled up with a few people inside. A tall kid, about 16 or 17, climbed out. I felt startled and nervous. He came up to me and said "Hey, I'm looking to buy a skateboard. Yours looks pretty cool. Can I try it out?" I wanted to say "no," take my board, and run into my house. But another part of me

3

wanted to be polite and still wanted to trust people. I hesitantly put my board on the street. The kid jumped on it, rode it for a few second, skated toward his car, picked it up, and jumped in the car with it. The vehicle sped off with a screech. I broke down and ran into the house. I was mad my friends didn't protect me or run after the car. *I felt stupid, taken advantage of.*

I gave up skateboarding and began collecting comic books. I felt this was a safer hobby because I could keep the comics in my house. I read most of them but collected more for the sense of pride, security and control I felt as my collection grew in size and value. But I remember feeling competitive with my friend Michael who had a better comic collection.

One day my school friend Anthony came over to look at my comics, maybe trade a few. Afterward, we went downstairs. He said he needed to use the bathroom. I told him there was a bathroom downstairs but he wanted to go upstairs. I felt it was kind of strange but let him go. When he left, I ran upstairs to check my comics and found a valuable one missing. I ran down the block, caught him and yelled: "Did you take my comic book?" He denied it! "Well, it was there a minute ago!" I accused. He still denied it. I called his bluff and asked him if I could look at his comics. He showed them to me and there was my comic book. I yelled "That's my comic book!" He shot back: "That's my comic book."

I was stunned. I wanted to hit him and take it back but I wasn't a fighter. I kept asking, finally begging, for it back. He told me he'd sell it to me for a dollar. I was outraged at having to pay to get my own comic back. It was as if he was holding it hostage.

I asked him to come back to my house so I could get the money. I planned to tell my Mom, sure she'd help get the comic book for me like she helped get my skateboard back. I told her the situation but she told me: "Terry, here's a dollar.

4

Get your comic book back and don't ever let him back in the house. He's not your friend." I felt let down. I wanted her to help fight my battles. I was on my own. I paid Anthony his ransom. It was humiliating. I grabbed my comic book and yelled "Don't ever come back!"

I felt victimized, powerless. That's when I started not to trust people. I couldn't trust my Dad to not drink or to pay child support, I couldn't trust my Mom to fight my battles, I couldn't trust strangers, I couldn't trust my friends. These incidents contributed to my shoplifting. I needed to be the perpetrator and get back my lost power. I needed to be on other side of the fence to experience what it was like to take rather than be taken from. *And I did...*

I began stealing comics at comic book conventions. *I felt entitled to do so to even the score.* It wasn't anything I sat down and contemplated or planned. I bought a few, stole a few by a bit of slight of hand. I got away with it a couple times over several months. I recall the guilty thrill of coming home and laying out my bounty on my bed. *The stolen comics took special significance compared to the ones I'd purchased.*

But I was a novice and was caught. One of the comic book dealers saw me and asked to see my pile of comics, as I had asked to see my friend's. She threatened to call security. Unlike my "friend," I didn't have the nerve to play hardball; I started crying, pleading with her. I ended up paying for the comic book. I shuffled out to the lobby, sat in my chair trembling. When my Dad came to pick me up, I didn't tell him about it. I was shaken up. My stealing halted but I still felt powerless.

My interest in comics quickly waned as another kid from my neighborhood, Sonny, came by wanting to trade. He came from a disreputable family. I didn't trust him and wasn't into comics anymore. I told him my friend Keith collected

5

comics, he lived a few blocks away. A few days later, Keith phoned me, screaming, asking me why I sent Sonny over. Keith's house had been broken into, most of his comics had been stolen. I felt terrible. All I could say was, "I'm sorry."

The police came to talk to me the following day. They asked me if I had any involvement in the break-in and wanted me to go to the station with them. I was terrified. I called my Dad, who was a lawyer, to come with me. I told him what happened but he didn't seem to believe me. I didn't know why. This really hurt me. I was a good, trustworthy kid but I had a guilty conscience from my stealing at the comic conventions.

The police interviewed me. I was never contacted again and never found out if they charged anybody with the burglary. Keith stopped being my friend after that. I began to sell my comics at garage sales and at comic book conventions where I rented sales tables.

My relationship with my Dad continued to be strained. He never apologized or took responsibility for the effects his drinking and the divorce had on me. He spent money lavishly, trying to buy my love; other times he withheld money, as if to punish me. I wasn't able to express my feelings directly but they were always underneath: the anger, the disappointment, the sadness. I'd show it by being quiet, not talking to him, not going out with him when he wanted to pick-up me and my brother. I was embarrassed by him. He was overweight. He'd get tipsy, act boisterous in public. He always drew attention to himself. I was ashamed of him. He got the message but didn't seem to care. I wanted to love him, forgive him. I couldn't.

In junior high school I immersed myself in school and in sports. I kept out of trouble, tried to be the opposite of my father by being reliable, sensitive, helpful, considerate. I took my anger out on Jordy. I became enraged at him when he didn't do what I said. I felt I deserved respect. I hit him, yelled at him, teased him. I regretted this and have told him many times how sorry I am. Today we have a better relationship but it took a lot of work. I still have to be careful about criticizing him, giving him unsolicited advice, or expecting him to be like me.

By my mid teens, I became interested in girls. But despite being physically fit, tough-minded and outgoing, I was shy and insecure around them. I feared rejection and was afraid of betraying an unspoken loyalty toward my mother. I'm sure I also felt the intense shame of being the son of an alcoholic, I had no male role model.

My Dad remarried around this time. He had been dating this woman from Iran who was studying to be a nurse. I felt uneasy about the marriage, though she was nice to me. A few months later, my Dad told me they were going to have a baby. This made me extremely anxious. I was afraid neither he nor my step-mom would be able to care for a child. He proved that to me already. My fear was one day I'll have to be responsible for that child, too. It was going to complicate my life.

By high school, I was barely holding things together but nobody would have guessed. I was still insecure. I coped as well as I could by focusing on school and sports. I tried to find where I belonged, where I fit in. I had a few friends, I tried marijuana and alcohol. Chemicals never did much for me. I still had faith if I was a nice guy, kept my nose to the grindstone, played by the rules, things would work out: I'd be acknowledged, girls would like me, I'd be happy, life would go smoothly. What I wanted was my Dad to acknowledge me. I wanted my Dad to stop drinking and get his life together. I wanted him to care about me. *However, what I wanted I didn't have control over.*

I got my idea about what a man should be from the things

my Mom said she didn't like about my Dad. But my Dad was in me. If he was bad, then wasn't I? I knew the bad aspects weren't the whole picture. He was talented, funny, smart, creative. My love-hate relationship with my father was confusing and heart-breaking.

During high school I gravitated toward art and planned on going to an art college when I graduated. My mother was talented in art and she encouraged me. I also started playing more piano and guitar--sports became less prominent in my life. My senior year, I fell in love with Sally, a junior: blond hair, blue eyes, popular. She was a music major, played the harp and piano. This reminded me of my Dad. I had a part-time job at a movie theater and a loud '78 Firebird I'd bought. *Things were finally going my way. I felt on top of the world!*

then the bottom fell out

The next few months I felt like a plague had fallen upon me. My face broke out with a severe case of acne. A few weeks later, my girlfriend broke up with me. I thought she left me because of my acne but learned from a mutual friend that she got bored with me. I thought I was a perfect gentleman, a romantic. To hear I was boring was a blow to my ego. Her breaking up with me felt like the straw that broke the camel's back. My self-esteem plummeted. I cracked.

During this time, I rapidly lost interest in art. I should have used art as my salvation but it didn't work that way. I felt the added anxiety of not knowing what I would study after graduating. Art college didn't seem attractive anymore. Still, I continued to shop at this particular local art supply store a few miles from my home for the supplies I still needed for my classes. The store was owned and run by a man named Herb who had cerebral palsy. He pushed himself around the store in a wheelchair. His mind was sharp and I shopped there because the prices were good and because I admired him.

I started to steal from his store. Maybe I felt conflicted just being in there. Maybe he reminded me of how I felt: deformed. Maybe he reminded me of how powerless I was. Maybe I stole from that store because I thought I could get away with it: he couldn't catch me because of his condition. I suppose I took advantage of him just as I had been taken advantage of. Maybe I was trying to get my power back.

When I shoplifted, I got a high. It was a way of expressing, acting out my feelings, whatever big issues I couldn't make sense of. The stealing was an expression of frustration over my recent losses, a way of tipping the scales back in balance, a way of trying to make things right for me.

I felt guilty afterwards, I mean, here I was stealing from a man in a wheelchair. It wasn't like me to do something like this. Some other part of me took over. You think I would have stopped due to the guilt but I had all these feelings that weren't getting dealt with and shoplifting was like my release valve. But things kept going downhill.

I got fired from my job tearing tickets at the movie theater. The manager, Mr. Budley, told me,"Son, you've run out of juice." He was right. I was depressed. Shortly afterward, I developed an acute, mysterious lower back pain and stiffness so severe I had to crawl out of bed in the morning to get to my hot shower.

I barely made it through my final year of high school. I was so depressed I skipped school. One time my mother caught me coming back home after I left in the morning. I thought she would be gone to work. She took me to a psychologist, Dr. Wickett. I was very resistant. He wanted to go into my life's history; my focus was on the present and all the things going on. *I didn't tell him about my shoplifting.* I stopped seeing him--I only saw him three times--after I found out I was accepted to the University of Michigan. My spirits lifted a bit as I saw a new adventure ahead, a chance to start fresh.

Slowly, I stopped shoplifting, got over my breakup, and my acne cleared a bit but left some residual scarring. Again, I hoped things would get better and I'd find some happiness, some ease, some fairness. I was angry with my father because he refused to help pay for my college. His line of reasoning was if he paid for my schooling, I'd take it for granted and not do as well. He reminded me he paid for his own schooling. After all I'd been through, it was like a slap in the face! My Mom had just gone into business for herself and didn't have a lot of money. She was getting ready to move from Detroit to the suburbs so I would be losing my childhood home. I took out student loans.

When I got to college it was a culture shock. I came from a big city and high school but the university was bigger. I was aware of how many students came from wealthier backgrounds than I had. They had nicer clothes, more money. There were cliques. I was no longer part of the popular crowd. I tried not to show it but I felt inferior, inadequate, competitive. I thought college would be different. I didn't shoplift for a while but, again, I felt I wasn't getting what I wanted. Everything was a struggle. My grades weren't as good as high school because college was a lot harder and I felt ill-prepared. I still wasn't having romantic success. I started to hang out with a clique of "outsiders" in the dorm who were cynical and embittered which began to rub off on me.

One of my friends from high school, David, was in this crowd with me. He attracted women left and right. He was African-American, dressed trendy and carried a secret journal-sketch book wherever he went. Dave would always be there to laugh at my naiveté when I showed any trust in life being fair. He was a modern day existentialist. I still played by the rules but was becoming angrier inside.

10

Toward the end of the my sophomore year I applied at a few dorms for a job as a resident advisor. I felt I would make a good leader and counselor for other students and the job came with free room and board which would save me several thousand dollars a year. I was conscious about saving money as I was nervous about how I'd pay my loans back when I graduated. I didn't get the job, Dave did. I was hurt. I felt I was much more qualified and interested in the job, that he was just in it for the money. I felt, frankly, they chose him because he was African-American. I believe in diversity yet felt discriminated against. *The camel's back was weakening.*

I moved into a student co-op for my last two years of college. My friend Josh lived there and I had hoped to room with him but he chose to live with somebody else. That hurt. I didn't want to keep taking out loans for my living expenses so I got jobs at a student bookstore and a little deli in the Student Union building. Within a short time, I realized some of the employees were stealing. I started to become aware of opportunities to get things without paying for them. I started off buying books and food using my employee discount but then I crossed a line. I started to steal a book here, some food there. Little by little, it escalated. *I got a rush by getting something extra. I felt like I was helping myself, like I was taking care of myself in a way life was not. I felt a sense of entitlement. I couldn't be perfect or, at least, tired of trying to be. Little by little it started to peck away.*

One day, I asked out a young woman who worked at the deli. Her name was Sherri, she was in a sorority, so I felt I was taking a big risk. We went on a couple of dates. I thought things were going well. Abruptly, she decided she didn't want to go out with me again. I felt rejected, angry, and sad. It was hard working with her after that. It reminded me of my break-up with Sally three years earlier.

Shortly after the break-up, I was working at the deli. It was lunch hour, very busy. A customer asked me for a sandwich from the pre-made sandwich counter. I gave it to her--told her it was $3.00--and told her to go to the cash register to pay for it. She ran off, throwing three dollars at me. I took the three dollars and put it in my apron, intending to put the money in the register later. I went back to making sandwiches when it occurred to me: "I could keep this three dollars, it's no big deal. Nobody's gonna miss it. I deserve it. I'm a good employee." *That day a little fire was lit.*

Then, one little thing at a time--click, click, click, click-- I got these ideas of ways to take things to make myself feel better, give myself more. There was an element of greed there, I'm sure, but it was more about easing my hurt and anger. *It snowballed beyond what I intended.*

I stole more food and, when I worked the cash register, discovered ways to take money out of the drawer. I overstepped another line. I shocked myself. But it was as if a floodgate opened. It was easy, I rationalized it--"well, they're making enough money, we're not getting paid enough, all I've suffered in life, I deserve something extra."

It was contagious.

I developed the ability to pretend everything was okay in my life. I held things in, everybody thought I was strong. I developed the ability to put on an act and now I was taking it a step further. I would steal, put on an act, and nobody would suspect me.

Mainly, I stole for the feeling of getting something back. But money, food, or whatever I stole turned out to be a weak substitute for what I really wanted--love, appreciation, to be rewarded in life. I couldn't get that. I couldn't force people to give it me. So, I would take what I could for myself.

As time went on, I took more money, more food, more

books. I became more and more daring. I needed to steal more and more to achieve the same feeling, the same "high." Eventually, I turned to shoplifting again. First, I started taking chopped walnuts out of a bin in a store. I fed them to the squirrels who'd come up to me and take them from my hand. I felt a bond with squirrels because they know how to conserve, burying their food. I shoplifted other items-- toiletries, cassette tapes, mostly--and it became a daily habit.

my first arrest

The first time I was arrested was in 1986. I was 21. I didn't really know about security systems--I had stolen some cassettes from the store before and nothing happened. But this time the electronic gate went "beep, beep, beep." I knew I'd been caught. I stood there, frozen. A woman came running toward me. I tried to get rid of the cassette but it fell to the floor and she saw it. She pulled me to the back of the store and went to a nearby room to call the police. She called a young guy, an employee, to keep an eye on me. I remember him telling me "don't worry, it's happened to me before." This comforted me a bit but I didn't know what was going to happen next. I was terrified and ashamed.

A police officer arrived, took down my information, and gave me a court date. I didn't know what to do. Did I need a lawyer? I didn't tell anyone, not my family not a friend. I ended up going to court and they offered me and other first-time offenders a deal: keep out of trouble for six months and nothing would go on my record. I didn't need a lawyer for that. I pled guilty, paid the fine, and did my community service. A probation officer recommended I see a counselor but I didn't want or think I needed to. I thought I was just going through a phase.

I did my community service at the University Children's Hospital where I had previously volunteered when I was a freshman. I saw all kinds of sad things there: children born with birth defects, children who had traumatic injuries, diseases. Some kids died there. I went twice a week. I played with them, talked to them. You'd think I would have learned something from this experience but it seemed to ignite the part of me that felt that life was unfair. I'd go there and feel good while I was helping but each time I left I felt this terrible sadness and anger. Then I beat up myself emotionally because I wasn't able to appreciate what I had in life.

I didn't shoplift during my six month probation and I whittled down the stealing I was doing at my jobs. In my mind they were two different things--shoplifting and employee theft. Shoplifting was more serious. I could get arrested for shoplifting--and had--whereas the worst that could happen if my job caught me was I'd get fired.

Eventually I was laid off from the bookstore job and fired from the deli job because I didn't work any shifts during final exams. I think they were on to me at the deli anyway--about the stealing--so I felt my time was up. But I was upset. There went my opportunity to take food, money, books anything. I took an honest job in a local dorm cafeteria where there was little opportunity to steal--I didn't have access to any money or items that tempted me. In time I felt good about the opportunity to stop stealing, turn over a new leaf.

i was like a horse ready to break out of the gate

When my probation ended, however, I was back out there shoplifting. I was like a horse ready to break out of the gate. I was more alert to security systems and found ways to remove electronic tags, how to go the extra mile. *Fear had deterred me for a while but I had underestimated the problem once again.*

Life was pressing down on me. I was preparing to graduate

and didn't know what I was going to do for money, for a living. I was bored with school and wasn't having any luck with women. My time was spent stealing and shoplifting, or thinking about it and how to avoid getting caught. I majored in English Literature and thought about teaching. But I felt unstable and hypocritical. I didn't feel I could be a role model or teach anything.

Then, just before I graduated, I met a woman. Her name was Juniper. She was the most sweet and down to earth person. I had little money to spend on her. I felt desperate. I shoplifted several gifts for her and shoplifted for myself so I'd have extra money to go on dates together. I admired her goodness but my secret dishonesty created a wall between us. I kept telling myself: "Stop stealing. You can't be in a good relationship with her like this." But the other side of me was stronger.

In a way, the shoplifting gave me an edge because my biggest fear was being rejected for being boring or too good. In my mind, stealing made me "a bad boy," albeit a secret bad boy. It began to weave its way into my personality. It seemed to give me depth. I was capable of walking both sides of the track. But I didn't anticipate how much it would envelope me.

Some people seemed as if they were either too good or too bad, one-dimensional and shallow. I despised people like this. I took a pride in having a secret life. It made me feel powerful. When life wasn't going my way, stealing was my way of lashing out. Almost every new day brought some new unfairness.

My relationship with Juniper brought me new joys which eventually slowed down my shoplifting. I had moments of clarity when I realized it was wrong and was affecting me. I suffered from guilt, shame, depression, anxiety. I'd stop for a while and focus on what I appreciated in my life. But it never lasted for long. *Something always drew me back to stealing.*

I graduated from college two months after meeting Juniper and, with a couple of friends, took a trip to Europe for six weeks. After the first week, I went my own way. I stole two or three times in Europe--small things, like food, from stores. All in all, I rarely felt tempted to shoplift. I felt healthy, alive, adventurous, content. I loved the feeling of living on the edge, being a scavenger, a survivor, sleeping in parks, on beaches, on trains, relying on the generosity of strangers. I'm not sure where this came from because when I was younger I didn't like having to scrounge. But it did seem to keep us together as a family. It felt good to know I could survive if I needed to.

When I got back home, my fantasy life of freedom had burst: I was broke and had to move back home with my Mom. I had a degree from a top university but was lost and depressed. I didn't know what I was going to do with my life. I still had a relationship with Juniper but sensed she was losing interest in me. I felt like a loser. I got a job at a restaurant as a salad maker. Sometimes I made Greek salads, wrapped them up, and sneaked them to my car. I barely made ends meet. I returned to shoplifting to take my mind of my life, get something back, a rush, a high, to kill the pain.

I next took a job as a waiter where I made a little more money. My self-esteem inched up but I knew it still wasn't what I was capable of. Eventually I found ways to steal a little food and money from that job, too. I was getting out of control again and didn't know how to slow myself down. I was in a rut.

After nearly a year of drifting, my father persuaded me to apply to law school. He had stopped drinking--even if doing it on his own--and was getting his life back together. We started to get closer. But I didn't want to go to law school. I didn't want to be an attorney. I didn't want all that pressure.

16

Secretly, I blamed my Dad's drinking on his being a lawyer rather than doing something he really loved. He almost went into music but, my mother told me, his parents thought being a lawyer would be more stable for a family life. I knew I had to find what made me happy.

But at this point in my life I felt I had no options except law school. I felt it would be a way of bonding with my Dad. I took out more student loans and wasn't happy about that. In late 1988 I began my first year at Detroit College of Law. I moved into a small apartment downtown. It was a rat hole but I was ready to move out of my Mom's.

Again, I turned over a new leaf, still nurtured the hope that life would work out. I saw my shoplifting as a reaction to things not working out and, in a strange way, it also became my handy excuse why things continued not to work out. I believed part of why things didn't work for me was that I was shoplifting, like it was some sort of karma or punishment. If things didn't go my way, I blamed it on my shoplifting. Shoplifting was my scapegoat. And if things went my way while I was shoplifting, I felt even better, like I was unusually lucky. It was my attempt to control life. But my sense of control was an illusion.

I told myself I wouldn't shoplift once I got into law school. I knew it would be pointless and hypocritical to study the law and break it at the same time. My classes were hard but interesting. I didn't know anybody but I felt I was fitting in. I was known as the guy with the tattered blue jeans because most of the students were better dressed and from wealthier backgrounds. I prided myself on being unique. I was friendly, though, and people wanted to get to know me. Things were really going well.

then life happened

It was late Halloween night and I was at my Dad's house.

Earlier we went trick-or-treating with my 8-year old half-brother Sammy. It was a wonderful evening. I felt closer to my Dad than I had in years. It seemed he was getting healthier, happier. But later that evening, when everyone was asleep, he woke up in the middle of the night: he had a stroke My step mom, Rezi, drove him to the hospital. I felt like a scared little boy, confused, helpless.

When I got to the hospital early in the morning I found out how severe the stroke was. He was unconscious and they didn't know if they could save him. *My whole world turned upside down.* The doctors told us they could perform some surgery to try to save him but, even if they did, it was likely he'd have severe brain damage. *I remember the terror of not knowing what to do.* My brother Jordy arrived and both he and Rezi looked to me to make that tough decision. I had to be the adult and I decided we had to try everything to save his life. I didn't want to regret not trying everything.

They did the operation and saved him. He awoke up from his coma a few days after the surgery. I kept a vigil by his bedside. In some way it comforted me to see him lying there, controlled, taken care of. I visited him every other day. He had a lot of brain damage.

I moved out of my apartment and into his house, near the hospital, to comfort Rezi and Sammy. It was a familiar role, a familiar feeling but I wanted to be free to live my own life. I wanted to scream! I felt obligated to help, resentful about having to help. I knew I'd feel guilty if I didn't help. I felt trapped. I became angry at God, angry at life. Everything had been going my way and then--boom! It was gone. *I was ready to snap.*

Shortly after my Dad's stroke, I started shoplifting again. He got out of the hospital after five months. He was in a wheelchair. We all tried to stay patient and positive. We hoped he would walk again. He was only 49 years old. I remember breaking down in tears with some friends at a party. A friend pounded a pillow for me, chanting: "It's not fair."

I muddled my way through law school, my concentration and stride broken. I thought of dropping out but where would I go? What would I do? I told very few people about my Dad's illness. *It was hard for me to be vulnerable and I was wary of looking for pity though, secretly, I guess I wanted that.* I looked at the students and imagined how easy they had it, how easy their lives were compared to mine.

Juniper and I were still seeing each other but it was strained. The pressure of keeping it a secret had become too much. Prior to my second year of law school, I decided to tell her about my shoplifting. I didn't think she'd leave me because of it and I naively thought I'd stop shoplifting if I let my secret out. I said: "I have something important to tell you. I've had this problem the last few years. I've got a problem with shoplifting." Juniper looked at me not with shock or surprise but with relief. She said "I knew something was going on with you, Ter. I wondered about some of those gifts, and your Sunday paper routine." I used to swipe the Sunday newspapers from storefronts on my early morning walks and bring them back to her and her house mates like some weekly Santa Claus.

She informed me that she had a secret of her own. She, too, was dealing with her own issues. The difference was, she was in counseling. She told me to get some help. My telling her was a first step but I was terrified of giving up shoplifting. It had become my shield and my sword, my defense to life's pains. I wasn't ready to lay my weapons down. I wasn't ready to surrender.

My second year of law school began in late '89. I took a job at the law school library to help pay my bills and to keep occupied. Without looking for them, I found opportunities to take things, an office supply here, some change there. The whole cycle started again. It seemed to help me get by, not unlike somebody needing a drink.

During this period there were several times I was caught by store owners. Each time, instead of calling the police, they just let me go. I'd be momentarily grateful and tell myself: "I've got to stop." But my decision was not a decision at all. It wasn't a matter of choice any longer. Soon I was shoplifting daily. It was as if I was possessed. I felt compelled to continue until something stopped me.

i hit a bottom

By March of 1990 it became clear that my Dad wasn't going to walk again. I didn't know if I wanted to be a lawyer. I didn't know if I could be a lawyer. My relationship with Juniper was strained because I wouldn't seek counseling. I ended up committing an infidelity with a mutual friend of ours. We broke up. I knew that my Dad had affairs during his marriage to my Mom. It shocked me that I was capable of doing that. *My world was crumbling. I knew I needed help.*

It was at this point that I told my Mom and Dad I needed to see a counselor. I told them I was depressed. I told them I'd been shoplifting for the last several years. They were shocked but both were supportive. My Mom said she had a feeling something was going on. She thought it was drugs. My Dad was clueless because of his condition. They knew I was a good person, believed it must be more of an emotional problem. I started seeing a psychologist, Dr. Ebner. There was a ray of hope.

But a week later, my Mom went out of town. I'd seen my new counselor once but was still unstable. I was feeling down and all alone. I got this idea to try to get back with my girlfriend. I felt desperate, restless. My thoughts took over...

*I can't stand it! What have I done? I hate my life! Pain...
there's only pain! Nothing's fair. I didn't mean to hurt her. I
didn't mean to fuck things up. I can't believe my life has
come to this. I can't sit still. I can't stay here. I've gotta do
something. What?... I'll make it up to her. Yeah. I wish I
could take her out to dinner tonight. I wish she'd forgive me.
I could go to the supermarket and get something... maybe a
bottle of champagne, like the one I took before. That'll be
romantic. That'll show her you love her. Can't sit still. This
is torture!*

*Just do it! Grab your trench coat, the long one. Saturday
morning's are pretty busy there, no one will notice. Bring
some cans back. I'll just go, get it, and come home...*

*Okay, we're here. Just act calm. You know the trick.
Walking... through... the doors... Okay, I'm in. Look
around... Everything looks okay. Act normal. Go to the bottle
return and get the receipt. Act friendly. Smile... Okay, got the
receipt. Don't browse too long. Just go to the champagne
aisle. Walking... slower! Okay, we're here. Nobody's
watching... Which one should I get? Where's the expensive
stuff, the stuff I took last time? Shit! All they've got is the
cheap ones! Well, I'm already here... This one'll do... wait!
Look around. Act normal... Okay, looks clear. Take the bottle
and slip it inside your coat... Act like you're still looking for
something... Okay... Get out of here...*

*Go to the check-out line to get your change for your cans
and bottles... Fifty cents... Might as well grab a pack of
cigarettes here. Yeah, put them in the pocket... Man, it's
kinda warm in here. Hey, hold the bottle inside your
coat–it's slipping! Don't let it fall, calm... Oh, man, it's
bulging out! Stay calm! Okay, give the cashier your receipt...
Okay, take the money and say thank you: "Thank you." Now,
hey, where'd the bag boy go? Okay, stay calm, just walk
out... Who are those two guys at the door? Oh shit, I'm*

screwed! Keep calm...

"Excuse me, sir. Could you come with us?"

Somebody shoot me... I want to die...

The two men roughly escorted me to a small room near the exit. I was shaking, in tears. They told me they'd been waiting for me to come back to the store, that they suspected me before. I cried and told them I was seeing a counselor. They said: "We don't care. Shut up!" They asked for the bottle. I gave it to them. The cigarettes fell out of my pocket, too. They asked if I had any money on me. I told them yes, about twenty dollars. They looked at me with disgust, telling me: "You don't have any reason to shoplift!"

A policeman came and walked me out of the store. I kept my head down, shaking, hoping nobody recognized me. I'd never been in a police car. I began to panic as I realized I had a small amount of marijuana in my coat pocket. I hardly ever smoked but it was probably poetic justice for all the other times I had gotten away with shoplifting. I was fingerprinted, photographed. *It was humiliating. And, yet, there was this tremendous sense of relief, like finally someone took control of me. I felt like a little child being guided, following orders.*

When my Mom came home-a few days before her birthday-it was so hard to tell her about my arrest but I knew I had to. "Mom, I have something to tell you..." It was as if I had hit her in the stomach. She clutched her abdomen and bent forward, stumbling toward the bathroom, choking, coughing. I felt so ashamed that I had hurt her. Some birthday present.

I continued in therapy with Dr. Ebner and waited nervously to be contacted about my arrest. It was a month before a detective called to say I was being formally charged. I hired a lawyer and over the next three months I felt like my life was in limbo. *It was nerve-racking.* I was mainly concerned with how this arrest would impact my ability to graduate law school and practice law.

Eventually, I got a plea bargain. I didn't do any jail time but was on probation for six months, paid a fine and did community service. I felt a great sense of relief. I was determined not to take this shoplifting thing as lightly as I had done four years earlier.

Finally, in therapy, I started addressing the underlying issues which contributed to my starting shoplifting: the anger toward my father, feelings of pressure for my over responsibility as a child and currently, the guilt over saying "no" to anything. I gradually gained insight into my behavior. Though I decreased my shoplifting I didn't stop it. Finally, Dr. Ebner suggested that I was addicted.

a light bulb went on

Addicted to shoplifting? That was the first time I considered this. I didn't know shoplifting could be addictive. I'd never heard that before. But it made perfect sense! There was a part of me that wanted to stop and a part of me that didn't. Part of me was afraid of living without it. It was the primary way I coped with life. With this awareness came the beautiful, frightening awareness that I was more like my father than I ever thought.

Being in therapy twice a week didn't make the pain go away. My pain got deeper. I hit walls of resistance and impatience. In the beginning I think Dr. Ebner felt he could cure me just by guiding me to an understanding about how I began stealing and why I continued. But it became clear that more was needed. I discovered why I'd begun shoplifting and why I was continuing to do so but that was only half the battle. Stopping it was a whole other issue. Letting go of the past was hard. I wanted the world to change, not me. I wanted my Dad to be well. I wanted to be free from the burdens of life. I wanted things to go my way for a change. I had no choice but to continue. Life would be too painful without my crutch.

Dr. Ebner and I looked for a group for recovering shoplifters. There were none. This made me feel isolated, more alone, more hopeless. There were support groups for every other addiction: alcohol, drugs, gambling, sex, eating, co-dependency. It wasn't fair.

Eventually, I was put on Lithium for a few months but that didn't change anything, neither my mood nor my behavior. My Dad was manic-depressive and had been on Lithium but always went off his medication. Our similarities stunned me. I was engaging in a self-destructive behavior except mine was shoplifting instead of drinking. I had highs and lows, too. *It was a shock to acknowledge this but a blessing because it created a link to my Dad, a link of compassion.* I always judged my Dad for his drinking and felt I was holier than thou, I was a better person. "I'd never do anything so self-destructive." I had to take a hard look at who I was.

Unlike my Dad, however, I was determined to break my cycle of madness. My Dad had stopped drinking but it was probably like the times I stopped shoplifting. He didn't go to counseling, he didn't go to A.A. I always got the feeling he was winging it. I wanted real change and knew I needed help.

I kept hitting walls six months into therapy, still hoping the world would change. I still shoplifted about once every other week. I was honest with Dr. Ebner about this. Then my health insurance ran out and I quickly built up a therapy bill which made me nervous. I started to shoplift more frequently. I told myself it was the only way to save the money I needed to pay for therapy. It became a Catch-22. I told Dr. Ebner about this. He seemed exasperated with my resistance and explanations. He discontinued our therapy. He told me: "This has become counterproductive. You need to find another way to stop. It's up to you now. I can't help you anymore." He was right.

I set my focus on keeping out of stores more and, therefore, stopped shoplifting for a while. I was getting close to graduating from law school and focused on my studies and the bar exam. I also joined a local blues and reggae band and played keyboard. After graduating, I got my first job as a law clerk at a reputable law firm in downtown Detroit. I knew one of the managing partners, Bill Goodman, my next door neighbor growing up. I moved back to my mother's temporarily. I took the bar exam and felt I had done well. But I had to wait.

a turning point

During this time I happened to see an article in the newspaper about a local support group called S.O.S. (Secular Organization for Sobriety), an alternative to Alcoholics Anonymous and Narcotics Anonymous. The group was primarily for alcoholics and drug addicts but touched on co-dependency as well. It took me three meetings to open up and tell the group about my shoplifting addiction. I feared I would be judged as different, as a thief. I noticed there were perplexed looks on a few faces but, overwhelmingly, I felt accepted. The group took me under their wing. I'd found a big part of what I was looking for.

In the interim, I saw two other therapists for brief periods of time. One, Dr. Brownfain, demanded I get rid of everything I had shoplifted. I didn't like that idea. He even suggested this to my mother who decided she was enabling me by allowing me to keep stolen items in her home. Her ultimatum: I had to get rid of anything stolen. I told her I was afraid if I got rid of anything I might go out and steal new things to replace the loss. I held on for dear life. I felt my stolen objects symbolized my pain, my struggle and, in some way, my success as a shoplifter. It wasn't easy to say good-bye to these things. "I don't want it in my house," she said. I thought to myself: "How is she going to know what I stole and what I didn't?" She obviously thought about this, too, because she told me that she had to trust me or she simply could demand that I get rid of *all* my books and cassettes.

I did my best and picked out the shoplifted cassette tapes and books from the ones I'd bought. I gathered about a hundred cassettes and several books. I offered to sell them but she didn't want me profiting from "stolen goods." She ended up donating them to charity. I was angry that she didn't even trust me to donate them myself. But who could blame her? I felt the void that was left by my loss but I kept focused on work, the band, therapy and S.O.S. meetings.

A week or two later, I got in a near fatal car accident. I was rushing home one night when I slammed into a turning car at an intersection a couple blocks from home. My car was totaled. I was taken to the hospital and kept overnight, lucky to have no injuries. I remember laying in the hospital bed feeling upset about the loss of my car, my loss of control, but grateful to be alive. I realized how fragile life was. I felt like I was being given another chance. I felt humbled. I didn't want to waste it.

I got a ticket for the accident and my insurance didn't pay for any of my car because it was my fault and my coverage was slim. I had to take the bus to and from work for several months. I'm surprised I didn't give in to shoplifting. I guess my recovery was starting to take root. Eventually, my Mom bought a new car and gave me her old one. Meanwhile, while waiting for my bar exam results, I went to work and came home and watched TV as a way of keeping out of stores. I went to S.O.S. meetings twice a week.

The envelope finally arrived from the State Bar. I said a prayer and opened it. I had passed my bar exam by the skin of my teeth! I was jubilant! I phoned everybody I knew and temporarily recognized the many people in my life who cared about me. My elation, however, was cut short when a day later, I got a notice I was being called before the State Bar Character And Fitness Committee. They needed to investigate my criminal record before approving my law license. *My heart sunk.*

I needed to talk to someone. I phoned an attorney who specialized in helping would-be lawyers and lawyers get or keep their licenses. He was pessimistic about my chances. "You've got a recent arrest for shoplifting--during law school of all times--and a marijuana charge along with it. That's two strikes against you. There's two things the State Bar worries about: dishonesty and substance abuse, and you've got both." I hung up the phone. *Was all my hard work about to be for nothing?*

I mustered the courage to confide in my boss, Bill. I stepped timidly into his office. He knew something was wrong. I told him about my passing the bar but this was the hard part. "I have to go before the Character and Fitness Committee," I told him. I sat down and started to sob. He asked me, with levity, "What was it: wine or women?" I told him "Neither. I was arrested for shoplifting." He didn't miss a beat in supporting me. I told him my history. He asked me if I was still shoplifting. I told him I was in therapy and going to a support group and that I hadn't shoplifted in several months. That seemed like a short time for him but an eternity for me. He told me he'd help me. I sighed and my entire body eased open.

Bill came with me to three meetings with the committee. Through letters from Drs. Ebner and Brownfain, and some persuasive arguing, we convinced them I did not have a substance abuse problem and was not shoplifting because of any inherent dishonesty but, rather, due to emotional problems and stress. I told them I had worked through most of the issues and would not hesitate to get back into therapy if I needed to. They narrowly approved me for my law license.

I felt a great honor and was sworn in as a member of the State Bar a few months later in January 1992. It truly felt like a gift, a miracle and I wanted to make the most of it. Both my mother and my father attended the ceremony. My mother cried, knowing what an ordeal it had been for me, for her. My father watched quietly from his wheelchair.

I continued my work as a law clerk for Bill's firm. I was reluctant to put myself under too much stress. I realized I still had a lot of room for growth. I fell into the same sad routine of going to work, coming home and watching TV. I continued to go to S.O.S. meetings.

In April I got a call from a friend who wanted me to take a weekend seminar called "The Forum." It was a spin-off of the *est* training which I had taken at age 15 while in high school. I thought to myself--"*been there, done that*"--but my friend's excitement drew me in. I knew I was in a rut and needed some kind of jump start. The *est* training challenged my beliefs and stories about my life and exposed what kept me stuck in the past. But I think I was too young to get it. I decided to attend a free introduction to "The Forum." I knew there was more to life than what I was experiencing. I signed up.

The course helped get me out of my shell. I started to meet new people and it occurred to me that I was still on the pity pot, still feeling like a victim and still feeling that life was unfair. *That old tape.* It gave me some breathing space to look at my life. I took a few more seminars and became more energized, more hopeful. I'd stopped shoplifting by this point but knew I still had to keep an eye on it. I was taking my life to the next level.

In July and August, I took the fourth and final seminar in the

28

main series, "Self-expression and Leadership." It got me to look at where I am and can be a leader in my life, what my passion is, what I'm good at, and what motivates me. Each participant was asked to create a project in his community which expressed his deepest and most authentic concern, passion or contribution. I remember racking my brain, asking myself: what can I give to the community, I don't have any passion? And then it hit me: I thought, "Right now, I'm passionate about my recovery and stopping shoplifting." Was this the opportunity to start the shoplifters recovery group I felt I still needed and which I was sure others could benefit from?

And so, C.A.S.A. (Cleptomaniacs And Shoplifters Anonymous) was born.

I did the footwork and, in September 1992, started the group. I secured a meeting room at the church I attended my S.O.S. meetings. A respected member of that group vouched for my character as I figured the church folks might be a little nervous about a recovering shoplifters group meeting in their building. To my surprise, they were very supportive.

Because I was a newly practicing attorney I sent notices to the courts but didn't put my name or phone number on the flyers because I was afraid of being associated with the group. I naively invited a newspaper reporter to our first meeting to help publicize our group but nobody showed up that first night. She interviewed me but wouldn't write a story about the group until there actually was a group. I begged her to write it so we could get the word out but she wouldn't.

i was ready to give up

For fourteen consecutive weeks I showed up on Wednesday nights. Nobody else did. I was ready to give up. I called a couple of the courts back to see why they weren't sending people to the group. One court clerk summed it up, saying "Oh, yeah, we got your notice but we thought it was a hoax. A group for shoplifters? And there was no name or phone number on it." I hit my head and realized I had to go out on a limb a lot more or give up.

The court clerk gave me the number of a local therapist who'd given a recent presentation on shoplifting for the courts. His name was Steve Campbell. I called and went to visit him. He was a tall trim man in his late 40's with a shock of whitish hair and a busy grey mustache. I felt at ease with him immediately. He was impressed with my story and my attempt to start a group. I realized I still had so much to work on emotionally. He introduced me to men's group work which became a big part of my life. I met men who were working on father issues, recovery issues, grief issues, life issues. I moved out of my mother's and into a house in a trendy part of town with three buddies. Juniper had moved back home out of state.

The day after Christmas, I managed to get an article about C.A.S.A. in the Detroit Free Press. They tied it into the holiday season and how there's a great increase in shoplifting and shoplifting arrests at that time of year. People began trickling into the group. Before long we had a core group of about five or six people. Finally, I met people who had the same problem I had. *It was the first time in my life that I felt good about helping others. And I was getting the help I needed.*

My Dad came to one meeting, in March '93. His assistant brought him in his wheelchair along with my brother Sammy who was 12. I wasn't happy about his bringing my brother. My Dad had little sense of appropriateness. There were about five or six other people at the meeting and I felt the familiar mix of pride and embarrassment over my Dad's presence. I felt like he was more there out of curiosity than support. At least he came.

the other shoe finally dropped

In April my Dad went to Europe with a friend to seek some alternative medical treatment for his stroke. I knew it was a bad idea and a long shot at best. He asked me to go with him but I couldn't. I had begun to distance myself from him over the last year as a matter of self-preservation. It was too painful for me to be around him. It was painful to say "no" and let go. He had given up hope of walking, starting drinking again, spent money lavishly, and argued with me when I expressed my concerns. He was away several days and as each day passed I felt more and more he wasn't coming back.

On a Monday night, I decided to visit my mother. I was quiet and asked if I could sleep over in my bedroom. The following morning I was in the bathroom shaving. I heard the phone ring. There was a noticeable silence. I stopped shaving and turned to open the bathroom door. My mother stood there with tears welling up in her eyes. My father had died. I took a deep breath and shook my head. The other shoe had finally dropped. My mother tried to comfort me but I had a wall up. I phoned my ex-girlfriend, Juniper, to tell her what happened. Within minutes I was choking back tears. Then, I got dressed and met a new friend of mine, a judge, for a planned lunch downtown. I was fortunate to have created a web of support within the last year. I needed it.

I was relieved my Dad was no longer in pain and I didn't have to worry about him anymore. But I was angry about the way he lived and the way he died. I dealt with this in therapy, in my men's groups, and in grief support groups. I kept in mind that I didn't want my life to end as his did. It is painful to say that but true. I wished he could have embraced recovery, a saner way of life, but he didn't or couldn't.

My Dad's death created a huge void in my life. I tried to fill it through more personal growth work and therapy. I went to seminars or support groups on average of four times a week. It was what I needed to stay connected and avoid shoplifting, or worse. I realized how co-dependent I was with my Dad and my family. I was always trying to save somebody. Now I was trying to save myself.

Yet, three months after my Dad's death, I found myself involved with a fairly needy divorced woman with three teenage kids. I'm sure I was filling the void and trying to rescue them in a way I felt I couldn't with my father. It was a stormy relationship which spanned, on and off, over four years. It was like a new addiction but I learned a lot through that relationship.

In 1994, I took a break from therapy. I felt stable and was getting a lot of support through C.A.S.A. and men's groups. I still saw my therapist in men's groups as he'd become a good friend. A week after I stopped seeing him he died of a heart attack. He was 52, a year younger than my father was when he died. I was in shock. My mentor was gone. It felt like a coming of age for me. There's a saying: "A boy really becomes a man when his father dies." I felt as if two fathers had died.

I wanted to follow in Steve's footsteps as a therapist. I stuck with C.A.S.A. and helped it grow. I realized how much I liked helping people, especially those who were open and ready for change but who needed the guidance and support to do so. From 1995-97 I went back to school full-time to earn my masters in social work. This was the first time in my life I really felt as if I knew what I wanted to do. I was dedicated to becoming a therapist.

In this period, I returned to Herb's Art Supply where I had begun my shoplifting twelve years earlier. I'd come back from a men's retreat weekend where I'd made a connection to my chronic lower back pain and stiffness which began around the time I started shoplifting there. I noticed that the store was going out of business. I asked to speak to Herb. The man in the wheelchair looked a little older and a bit more frail but was still vibrant and determined. I told him I had shopped at his store many years ago when I was in high school and I had shoplifted some things, that I wanted to apologize and tell him I didn't do it anymore, that I had started a group to help people who shoplifted. I told him that I admired him and that my Dad had been in a wheelchair and died recently. I offered to pay him for what I had stolen.

While I was talking, his body jerked and he gasped for air. I thought I had upset him. But as quickly as he contorted, he fell back at ease and said softly: "It's okay. I'm glad you got help and are helping others." His voice was as clear as I'd ever heard. I felt a huge relief. Again, I offered to pay him some money but he wouldn't accept it. I asked if I could give him a hug. He was open. I took a few short steps and slowly bent down. It was like hugging my father. "I'm sorry. I admire you."

I felt a peace come over me. I bought some fancy magic markers before I left. I felt a weight lifted from me. My back pain and stiffness eased a bit. I felt that was an important amend for me to make. In that case, I needed to take the risk to do it in person.

In 1997 I graduated from the University of Michigan with my Masters in Social Work. A friend of mine saw an ad in the paper for a substance abuse counselor at a holistic clinic. They asked me if I was in recovery myself. I was up front about my recovery from shoplifting during my initial interview and was happy they hired me. I felt luck was back on my side. I was passionate about that job though it had its challenges. Six months into it, one of my young clients overdosed from heroin and died. I was devastated. I felt guilty because I recognized my greenness and naivete caused me to miss some signs that he was in danger. I learned all new workers go through those feelings. I rebounded and kept learning.

After a year, I was promoted to Director as the clinic expanded. I thought long and hard about whether to take this opportunity. Why change? I was enjoying what I was doing and I didn't really want more pressure. It seemed like an old script: me being responsible for "the family." I don't know if I made the right decision or not but I decided I would regret not trying it. I wanted to see if I could dance with the responsibility in a different way.

It was a challenging job from the get-go. I was challenged by the clients, by management, and my co-workers. Talk about initiation by fire. Yet, I didn't give up. I helped redecorate the office, reviewed the client files, and got the company through a major audit to renew its three year accreditation. I was successful and felt like the hero.

A year later, I began feeling frustrated with my life. I had a job that was paying the bills so survival wasn't an issue. But it wasn't emotionally supportive. I rarely felt appreciated by my staff or by the management. Perhaps I didn't give that either. I was in a lonely place. Romantically, I was still longing to meet a woman who I could love with all my heart. I remember feeling angry that I wasn't rewarded with this. I'd paid my dues, done my personal growth work, stopped shoplifting, was contributing to humanity through C.A.S.A. and my career. "Where is she?!" I'd shake my fist toward the heavens. Without shoplifting as my numbing agent, I had to feel the pain and anger. At some point I had to let go because my misery was pushing people away.

Within a month after letting go, I connected with the woman

who would become my wife.

As my relationship with Tina deepened, my stress at my job did as well. I always had this longing for everything to be right: calm, stable and settled. I had the job but not the woman. Then I had the woman but began to hate my job. Something was missing. I felt as if I had hit a wall. From the outside it looked as if I had achieved everything: I was the Director of a recovery clinic--a noble mission--but another part of me had grown tired of saving the world, of being the king. I just wasn't having any fun. And this was taking its toll on my relationship as I could plainly see. I had a woman in my life who was opening me up to spiritual depths I had never experienced before and, yet, I felt spiritually dead.

I'd lost my mission.

Looking for some stability, I bought my first home in late 2000. Tina and I moved in together and became engaged. I left my job as Director on January 1, 2001. I needed to refocus and recharge. I ached to finish this book and to develop a private counseling practice. During this time, there were a number of high-profile shoplifting cases in Detroit which resulted in the deaths of the alleged shoplifters at the hands of security guards and in the chase. *It was the first time I realized shoplifting could result in death.*

I wrote an article for the Detroit Free Press about how these tragic events needed to be seen in a new light and outlined my story of addiction and recovery. I got radio interviews and phone calls from people in need. I began looking for a book publisher while I worked sporadically at three local counseling clinics.

Then, everything came to a halt. I ran out of money, I couldn't get my book published, the phone stopped ringing for interviews, and my work at the clinics was slow and uninspiring. Did I make a big mistake leaving my job? I felt on the verge of losing everything: my home, my fiancee, my career, my sanity. I was staring into the abyss. Taken by surprise, I'd felt my struggles were behind me. They had just begun.

Fortunately, my recovery foundation remained strong. I had the humility and presence to get back into counseling and reached out to my family and friends for support. My weekly C.A.S.A. group proved invaluable in "keeping me honest." As the founder and defacto leader of the group, it was humbling to need the support I'd become so accustomed to giving. But it worked. It was a miracle I didn't shoplift or steal during this stressful time. I never even thought about it as an option.

I went back to work part-time as a counselor at my former clinic to get some structure back in my life. I felt embarrassed to "return to the nest" after having failed to fly on my own. I later realized I needed to leave because I'd outgrown the pressures of the job: they didn't serve me anymore. The old script of being the hero had run its course. I was in transition but creating a new chapter in my life. It was exciting and scary.

The last two years have evolved slowly and methodically. I'd become complacent in my life when I bought a home and got engaged. I wanted to coast forever without the problems and stresses of my job as Director. I felt I'd paid my dues in life and done all the personal growth work necessary to deserve a long rest, and enjoy my new home, my new love. But I learned there will always be new challenges and I need to meet them by continuing to grow. This is life beyond shoplifting, where the real living begins. I love my wife and I love my life.

My recovery from shoplifting has been the constant, daily thread in my life during the last eleven years. But when

C.A.S.A. reached its ten year anniversary in late 2002, I was frustrated: nobody had started another meeting chapter and no publisher I contacted had faith in my book which I would have loved to publicize during the year-long Winona Ryder shoplifting case. But I did have five national television interviews, five radio interviews, and was quoted in at least several articles. "Thanks Winona!" Next time, do a "Magic Johnson" and own up to it. People will respect you more and you'll help ease a ton of shame for millions of others. It amazes me how *curious* an issue shoplifting addiction remains to most. I am encouraged, however, with the sincere interest I feel when I have the opportunity to make a difference by sharing my story. I hope to reach many more with this book.

Insights

I had early attention issues. I was jealous when my younger brother was born. I sought attention from a father who was unavailable due to his drinking. My mother's attention was divided. I sought comfort, validation, security. I discovered I could get this by being good, not making waves, helping others. However, this didn't satisfy me at the deepest level. I remained sad and angry underneath. Many children act out at a young age to get attention, I *acted in.* I put a lid on my feelings. *I was like a ticking bomb: it was a question of when I would go off. Shoplifting and stealing became my little explosions, my acting out in a desperate attempt to reclaim my lost childhood, lost father, lost family, lost freedom.* That's it in a nutshell. Keep it simple. My discoveries didn't immediately translate into my stopping shoplifting. But it got me to the doorstep of recovery, which has taught me more about myself each day.

Action Steps Toward Recovery
*Asking for help from my parents and/or others
*Continuing in therapy for nearly a year
*Tried medication
*Avoiding stores
*Sharing my secret with my boss, asking for help
*Focus on work for a while
*Attend S.O.S. meetings
*Take self-improvement seminars
*Start C.A.S.A.
*Went back into therapy for two years
*Became active in men's groups
*Attended grief support groups
*Went back to college to pursue my passion
*Worked through co-dependency
*Continued spiritual path through other groups and through tai chi, meditation, etc.

*Maintained attendance with C.A.S.A.
*Willing to take other risks (bought condo, left job, finish writing book)

<u>Danger Signs For Relapse</u>
*impatience
*overconfidence
*disappointment
*still feeling life is unfair (old script)
*dramatic loss
*money concerns

What parts of my story did you most identify with?

What new theories do you have about your life in relation to shoplifting or stealing?

What paths might you explore that you haven't already which may help you stop shoplifting, heal, and grow.

We all have our stories. Our life stories. Consider the ones that follow. How are we the same? How do we differ?

Marci's Story

Marci is an attractive woman, 40, energetic and articulate. She's been married for over ten years and has a boy and a girl, 7 and 10. She's an office manager for a law firm. Her marriage has been on the rocks for several years and she's been thinking of filing for divorce.

First, I want to say I'm excited I'm going to Florida for a week with a girlfriend and I'm not taking my husband or my kids--this is just for me! And I don't feel one ounce of guilt! I deserve this. My recovery from shoplifting has given me the strength to do this. It's been almost two years since I started coming to C.A.S.A. I could have never done this before. Never.

My earliest memory of shoplifting was when I was in elementary or middle school. It started with going to the stores and just switching price tags on items such as nail polish. I thought, "Well, that's not doing anything wrong, I'm still paying for it but just a different amount." *I was with friends and it was a thrill to see what I could get away with.* I knew deep inside it was wrong--I never even thought of it as shoplifting, just doing something wrong.

Around that time, my parents divorced. My mother remarried and my new father adopted me. I was rebellious and wanted to see my biological father. There was a lot going on. I don't know if my shoplifting was a cry for help or if I wanted to get caught. It makes sense now but it didn't at the time.

Then I stopped for a while and didn't start back up or even switch a price tag again for years. I got married and then my son was born. He was very sick. My marriage was starting to go bad--there was a lot of stress. This was about six or seven years ago. I was big-time shoplifting. I feel now it was a cry for help. "I'm going through so much I deserve this. I work and work and work and don't get anything." I didn't feel loved, I didn't feel appreciated or wanted. My self-esteem was low. My self-image was low. There was never financial fears. But there was more fear of the unknown: What's going to happen to my son? What's going to happen to me?

I typically shoplifted from grocery stores: toiletry-type items. It was completely planned. I literally had a list of things I was going to buy and things I was going to shoplift. I'd always buy something when I shoplifted, to kind of relieve my guilt. I remember gradually starting to think about stealing again and then doing it. My husband went grocery shopping and there'd be things he didn't buy that I wanted or needed. Things would add up and it just wasn't fair that his attitude was that "these things aren't truly necessary." I could always afford the things I shoplifted. *It was more an issue of getting away with it and a feeling like I had it coming to me. I've felt unappreciated almost all my life.*

Shoplifting made me feel better. It was the biggest high, the biggest rush. I've never felt the same feeling. *It's indescribable. But then there'd be a letdown afterwards. I don't know if it was guilt but I felt bad.* I knew it was wrong. I don't know if I felt guilty but I knew what I did was wrong. But I never tried to talk myself out of doing it until I started attending C.A.S.A. meetings. I didn't realize it became such a problem until the first time I got caught. But that didn't even stop me as I continued and got caught a second time. I feared, "Oh my God, this could jeopardize my relationship with my children, I've got to do something about this, this is out of control."

When I shoplifted, I'd hoard to the point that when I got home, I wouldn't even remember taking half the things I took. I even grabbed the wrong sizes. It became a compulsion. And it was almost always pre-planned.

The first time I was caught they didn't press charges and it scared me but obviously not enough. All they wanted was for me to buy the item. I never told anyone about this except my biological father who gave me the money. He didn't even say it was bad behavior. If he had given me a harder time, it might have helped me not do it again.

It's funny because my parents always bought me what I wanted when I was young. Neither one of them shoplifted. However, there was some minor dishonesty. My mother used to call them "white lies," little things like "you don't have to tell your Dad this" but I never really thought of them as lies until now.

Until recently, I'd always been plagued by feelings of inadequacy. I was an inadequate mother, an inadequate wife. I was very hard on myself, always blaming myself, you know, for what I could have done better. Now I've come to find out it wasn't all me.

Four years ago, I was arrested-officially-for the first time. I was in a department store, shoplifting clothes. Things were rough with my marriage. My husband didn't trust me charging things that I bought though I felt I needed them. I worked so hard, contributed so much of my paycheck. I had no control, no input. I had to ask him: "Can I have some money? Can I have the charge? Can I buy this? How many can I buy? When can I go?" I felt like an angry kid. It was like: "I'll show you, I'm going to get it anyway!" I used to talk myself into "I deserve this. This isn't fair. I'm going to get this one way or another." I felt sad and depressed, too.

When they caught me I remember feeling physically sick. My heart was racing and just about stopped when they said: "Please come with us." I had nightmares. It was terrifying. Getting caught was bad enough; having my husband find out was the worst. What am I worth now? Who's going to respect me? How am I going to respect myself?

The police came and took me to jail and I had to call my husband to get the kids, to get me out, to get an attorney. I started to think shoplifting was becoming a problem at that time. I thought "I'm a little out of control here," but I still wasn't a hundred percent convinced because there were times I didn't shoplift at all.

Getting arrested was the most shameful feeling in my entire life. I felt I was a terrible, terrible person. And my husband never asked me why. He just said "I can't believe you did that. How could you do such a stupid thing?" Those were his words. Then he asked "Have you done this before? How many times?" He was extremely demeaning, making my shame and guilt worse. I lied and told him this was the first time.

I was seeing a counselor prior to my arrest. I'd been in and out of counseling all my life, going back to age 10. But all the time I was in counseling I could never tell my psychiatrist, therapist, whatever, I was shoplifting. *This was my ultimate secret. I could talk about anything else but this.* It was always there. I never felt complete when I walked out of any session because I knew I was holding back. Eventually, I told my counselor but not until my self-esteem was better, when there wasn't so much guilt attached. Then I was able to discuss it. My therapist would say, "Well, I think it's an isolated thing and it's not really a problem," and I would say, "Well, it's not now but it really was." It took me a long time to get to admit that. *I felt it was such a taboo subject that I couldn't even tell my own therapist. I worried that I'd be looked at differently.*

After my arrest I stopped shoplifting for a couple of months. But then I picked it back up and was more cautious. I was more afraid, in a way, knowing what happens when you get caught. But I did it anyway. I obviously didn't have enough fear. I shoplifted usually no more than once or twice a week. But it was planned. I'd have a baby-sitter and on those days:

my days of seeing how much I could get. I'd say one percent was for myself, the rest was for my kids, the home-- everything from bedding to toiletries, cleaning supplies, kids' shoes. It wasn't that we couldn't afford it but it was such a fight with my husband to justify buying it that it wasn't worth the fight to me. I felt I had to have it. I don't know how much was truly needed. Did I really need that new comforter? None of it was truly a necessity. But I felt "why should I be denied? Why should I have to fight for it?"

But it took so much energy. I especially remember the days I had the baby-sitter. I'd leave five minutes after she arrived and come home five minutes before she'd leave and all I'd do in between was shoplift. I was physically and mentally exhausted. The fear, the breaking of the sweat, the taking the first load out to the car, the plotting and the planning and the looking around. It wore me out. Then hiding, ripping off the tags in my car, throwing them out the window so when I got home I could say "Oh, this isn't new, I've had this" or "I bought this a long time ago." *It took so much energy.*

Lying to my husband and having to keep track of the lies wasn't easy. Sometimes I'd call my mother to let her know I'd gotten the kids something in case my husband asked about it. My mother would cover for me, thinking I had bought things I didn't want my husband to know about right away. I never told her the truth.

A year went by and I got off probation. Two years later I was arrested again--that was almost two years ago. It's not that I didn't shoplift in between. The second time I was arrested, it was also planned. I had a list. I was going to buy some items, and steal some others, in a grocery store. I thought I was being careful but I got caught. It was different than the first time. I was angry at myself and I thought, "You really screwed up this time. Now nobody's ever going to believe that I'm capable of changing because this is number two."

I felt worse, more depressed. At least with my first arrest there were larger ticket items. This time it was toiletries for the house from the grocery store, such small items. I had the money in my wallet to pay for them. I really beat myself up. I had a harder time with it the second time than with the first.

Since that second arrest I haven't stolen one single solitary thing. Not a price tag, nothing. And I feel wonderful, fabulous, fantastic! It's great. I think, in a nutshell, I was soul-searching. I feel it was all meant to be. It was all a blessing in disguise. Though it was terrible, traumatic, shameful, I wouldn't change a thing. I learned so much. That's how I found out about C.A.S.A.

It's funny, I remember being scared to death before that first meeting. I thought there'd be very stereotypical criminals. I didn't think there'd be people like me. I was skeptical, thinking, "Yeah, this group of total strangers who can't even relate to me are going to help me." But I had to go. *After that first meeting I cried all the way home and said "Thank you God, this is what I've been looking for all my life. This is what I've needed. This all happened for a reason, to point me in this direction."* After that first meeting, I had no more nightmares about my arrest. I just felt a sense of comfort. Here's these people who understand. They've been there. There isn't anybody else on this earth who could identify with me. It was extremely comforting and reassuring.

The number one tool I've learned about is self-talk. If there's ever that urge I talk, even laugh, to myself: "You've got that urge? You've got to be kidding." I just walk and concentrate and focus when in a store. I usually bring just my wallet with me and leave my purse in the car--or at least not dump my purse out before I go in. I make sure I have enough money to get exactly what I need, just focus, and get out. I also try not to go to the stores unless I absolutely need to. I don't just look around or window shop.

I haven't had any recent urges to shoplift but I had a while ago. I'd get an urge to get something for my kids. I'd say "Oh, they could use that but it's so expensive." Then I'd immediately do some self-talk: "You don't really need it, they can get by without it." Sometimes I'd come home, be assertive and tell my husband: "Dammit, you're going to go and buy it or you're going to give me the charge card and I'm going to go and buy it!" I'm not going to give into this. *A huge part of my recovery has been speaking up for myself.*

My life isn't perfect but it's sure a lot better. Life in general may not be hunky-dory but I've never felt better about myself. Never. *I've finally forgiven myself.* That took a long time, a really long time. Instead of beating myself up and questioning myself about why I did such a dumb thing, I now say, "Okay, I did it. It was done. It's the past. Move on and learn from it. Just concentrate on that."

I've been fortunate to have family support. My mother knows, my father, one of my sisters--I don't know about the other--my parents told her. My mother, especially, has been extremely supportive. She remembers as a child growing up that her mother used to shoplift in front of her, and how embarrassed and humiliated she used to feel. I don't have a close relationship with my grandmother. I have a lot of issues with her and when I found that out it only made it worse. It felt good to be open with my mom and I am grateful that she didn't judge me. But telling my father was the hardest thing I've ever done. It was ten times harder than telling my husband. I always wanted him to be proud of me. I'm sure he felt disappointment which, I guess, I expected. But I feel he's seen me change and has been supportive.

I haven't told my children and I don't see any reason to do so. I don't want to tell them. I stress the importance of honesty and abiding by the law. When my son wanted something really bad and put it in his pocket, I went ten times more nuts than the average parent! I went on and on and on until he cried. I really scared him. "You could go to jail! You could spend the night! You could go to the bathroom and sleep on the floor!" I went into details which, obviously, he didn't know how I knew. But I got through to him.

My husband doesn't understand my shoplifting addiction any more than he did the day he first found out about it. But I think he finally has regained some respect for me because he hasn't thrown it in my face in a quite a while. For a while it was very hard. He'd say "Do I have to go with you?" He was very demeaning. I'd get angry but deep down inside I'd say to myself "Well, I guess you deserve it." Then I'd get to the point where I'd show him receipts: "Well, here, you want to see the receipts?" I guess he's picked up on my improved self-esteem, my solid recovery, because he's backed off. If I'm out shopping, every now and then he'll say "Be good." And that's okay. Back then if he had said it I would have resented it. Now, it's okay. It's a friendly reminder.

I still have many challenges ahead of me. I'm contemplating filing for divorce. And I'm scared. I know there will be custody issues with the children and I will need to be focused. Among other things, I need to focus on my recovery. I know my husband will bring up my shoplifting history. I guarantee he will. And I'm okay with that. I feel I can say to any judge: "That's the past. Yes, that was a part of my life but I'm over it. And how can you condemn me for the rest of my life? I've learned from my past." I used to be terrified. I feel so strong that I can look him in the eye and say "That was the past."

I will continue to need C.A.S.A.'s support. I enjoy the meetings anyway. I still benefit from them but most of all I feel I want to give back to the new people, give my little ideas that helped me and my little stories that may help someone else. I'm so grateful for all the help I got. I want to give back. It's also for myself. I made my amends. I paid my fines and costs to the courts. I've suffered all the stuff I've been through. I feel a little ashamed to say I don't feel any remorse towards what I did to the stores. And I still, at times, feel a little bad about how my shoplifting has affected my family.

Mostly, I just believe in myself whereas there have been others who believed in me but I didn't. Now, it's the other way around. I believe in myself and don't care who else believes in me. I mean, it's nice if it happens, but it's not needed like it was before. I was always looking for that appreciation, that approval--"You're kind, you're this, you're that"--well, now it's an extra if I get it but I'm sure not looking for it.

I'm more honest, more present, especially with my kids. I better understand the value of teaching them what things cost. "You just cut a hole in those pants, in those knees!" Before, I'd just go out and take another pair; now, "I paid $29 for that pair of jeans! What are you doing crawling on the floor? That's coming out of your allowance."

It still shocks me to think of the things I took, the risks I took. I can't believe I had the nerve, the gall. One time I stole a huge comforter right out of Hudson's. I walked right out with a three hundred dollar comforter. I can't believe I did that. It's like it was another person who did this. It wasn't spontaneous, it wasn't spur of the moment. I walked in there with all intent. It was like a different personality. But I really don't think it's there anymore. It may be so far down--I may have pushed it down--but I feel pretty clear. I'm not saying I'm never tempted or I don't have to be careful. There have been times where I'm shopping, I see something I like that I can't afford and I tell myself "Okay, get out of the store now, this is getting too tempting." I just take a deep breath. And when I get home I feel proud of myself, not disappointed like I used to feel when I hadn't taken something. Now I'm proud of myself that I didn't.

Insights

Marci realized the onset of her shoplifting as a teen, during her parents' divorce, was a cry for help. She acted out her feelings of fear, sadness and to distract, comfort, and soothe herself. She grew up in an environment where she was not allowed to express herself and did not feel appreciated. She was rebellious over not being able to see her biological father. She felt she was being treated like a little kid, a feeling replayed in her marriage.

She had been in therapy since the age of 10, yet, her shame prevented her from telling a therapist she shoplifted. She expressed great concern about how others viewed her. She always felt inadequate, and never believed in herself. Her self esteem was in the gutter.

Marci wanted to stop stealing but felt desperate and trapped. Her marriage deteriorated and she tried to survive emotionally. Shoplifting brought her momentary peace and the feeling of getting something back. She felt entitled to something more from life but had found few other ways to give to herself. Very little of what she shoplifted was for her. She tried to buy love and approval from others, especially her kids.

Action Steps Toward Recovery

*Assertiveness
*Forgiveness of self and others
*Self-talk in general and specifically when urges come
*Feeling good about being honest again
*Valuing self and not looking for others' approval
*Budgeting/delay of gratification
*Rewarding self (Florida trip, buying things)
*Staying out of stores
*Expressing her feelings

*Letting go of perfectionism
*Telling family members about her shoplifting to reduce shame/gain support

Danger Signs for Relapse

*Continued stress and breakdown in marriage
*Bitter divorce may bring pain and fear of change
*Her children find out about her history of shoplifting and she feels intense guilt and shame
*Return to economic survival mentality
*Not rewarding herself
*Dishonest behavior at work or having affairs
*Stopping C.A.S.A. meetings altogether (healthy fear and reminders may fade)

What parts of Marci's story did you most relate to or find informative?

Rick's Story

Rick is a professional man in his late 40's with a respected position in the community. He's been married for nearly 20 years. He has no children. His is a straight talker with a sharp intellect. He analyzes himself thoroughly yet, he recognizes, he needs to connect more with his feelings.

I've been attending C.A.S.A. for about eight months. I started the group about five days after my last arrest for shoplifting. It's not the first time I thought about attending. I had a previous "incident" and a counselor suggested I go to C.A.S.A., but for whatever reason, I chose not to. The resistance was still there. I just couldn't bring myself to do it. I denied the problem or I rationalized that whatever I was doing beforehand would be enough. It was too direct to deal with this issue.

I think I'm an obsessive-compulsive shoplifter because I've been behaving like this for a very long time, also because there's a physical feeling of panic, a sense of loss that needs to be replaced, a sense of a vacuum that needs to be filled. It can be completely irrational, whether it's needing an item by buying it, by stealing it. *The bottom line is: "I don't have that item and getting it makes me feel more complete."* That begs the question, why take it and not buy it? That's where all kinds of feelings come in.

I don't steal as a profession. I'm not a "booster." I don't sell what I steal. But, I've got to say there's a greed factor involved here. There's no question that part of my shoplifting has to do with getting away with something: *getting something for nothing, the sense of entitlement, filling other voids in my life, expressing anger.* There's no question those are big parts.

51

How I began shoplifting is a simple question with a complicated answer. I have to make a distinction here between shoplifting and stealing. When I was in second or third grade--I'll never forget this--I was with my mom at a five-and-ten store, and they had one large area with nickel and dime toys. I remember this as clearly as if it were yesterday. I wanted something and my mom said "No, you can't have it." And my mom wasn't big on denying me things. I remember throwing a tantrum in the store. I didn't get the item but the fact that I remember it this many years after left quite an impression and tells me how important having an item was--is--and what lengths I would go to get it and what kind of emotional buttons were being pushed.

I started shoplifting when I was ten or eleven years old. I remember going to a local store and taking a couple of magazines and comics. I got away with that for a little while before getting caught. They didn't tell my parents--a little slap on the wrist by the nice guy who was running the store. I felt frustrated but undeterred. I felt more scared of being caught or of being exposed but I don't remember feeling particularly ashamed, any more than I have ever felt to this day.

My shoplifting was completely spontaneous when it first started. Afterwards it became a focus of relief. My childhood was not the happiest. I had been uprooted from a pretty friendly environment to an isolated area. I really felt alone. I couldn't speak to my parents about it--they wouldn't have understood--at least that's what I felt. I didn't have many friends because it was a very isolated area. *Stealing became a way for me to expand my horizons, to live a little fuller life.* My focus was on the items I was taking that helped me expand my horizons, not so much on the taking itself. *But the taking resulted from everything else being so difficult.*

I shoplifted comic books, magazines, record albums. In and of themselves, the items weren't terribly significant. *But it was like someone who felt they were starving or dying of thirst, taking food or water in order to grow.* I felt I was in some kind of drought or poverty and this was the only way to meet my needs. I did whatever I could.

A major incident in my life occurred when I was in the second grade. I was with a group of classmates, boys, who were playing at recess. A lot of them had wads of baseball cards. They were playing some kind of game which involved trading the cards or piling up the cards, winning them somehow. I had a few cards but not that many. I found myself taking some of the cards off of the table, in play, in order to accumulate more cards for myself. I was noticed. And caught. I talked my way out of it by saying it was a mistake, I was holding them. But I knew the truth. I felt humiliated even though there were no repercussions. I expected them but there weren't. *I felt I'd gotten away with something and felt an enormous sense of relief. I wanted to belong. I wanted to have as many cards as I could to fit in with the group. I felt left out, so I was taking the cards in order to compete or feel as if I could be an equal. I felt inadequate.*

In my family, there was me and my brother who was six years older. In many ways we lived separate lives. *My parents were both Holocaust survivors.* They spent much of their time working either outside or inside the home. They were good parents but they didn't have role models themselves so they lacked some parenting skills. They did the best they could. My father was orphaned at an early age and had a survivor mentality. My mother's whole family was killed during the war. She somehow managed to survive and met my father right after the war. I'm sure most of our lives have been scarred by the war in ways we're not familiar with or aware of.

They didn't shower us with gifts. They basically gave us the message that if you needed anything all you had to do was ask. But it was frustrating because they didn't exactly encourage us to ask. If I did ask them for something, there was always that proviso that they had to understand the nature of the request. And what parent completely understands why a kid wants whatever? Sometimes a kid will want something because of social pressures or just because he wants it. Sometimes he wants it to feel special, feel distinct. So, the idea of having to go though them all the time to ask for something was very frustrating. I never had an allowance growing up. So the question was: "How the hell do I get stuff without having to go to Mom and Dad?

I can't remember if I ever saw my parents be dishonest but there was a culture of survival: *you don't necessarily break the rules, but you kind of bend them if it's a question of survival.* No one ever said anything to that effect but it was clear that stealing would not be understood or condoned. I learned many years later that *my Mom did have a shoplifting problem*, that she was caught and paid a fine. But this was years ago. Ever since learning that, it has filled in part of the blank. I must have seen her take something and it must've been something small--a food item.

After the war, she was engaged, as most people were, in some kind of activity, whether it was smuggling or whatever you want to call it, in which people did what they had to do to survive. *I can't emphasize enough the survivor mentality. I'm sure that shoplifting for me has been a survival skill.* That's what I grew up with. I've had to unlearn this and replace it with other attitudes. It hasn't been easy.

In our family, there was little permission to express feelings. There was a big lid on things, especially for me. My older brother was aggressive, assertive, an achiever. I grew up in his wake and it was tough being his brother. I think my brother's aggressiveness scared my parents and they decided their way of coping with me was to try to keep me in line by expressing the notion that I should just be a good boy and

54

that if I went along with the program, everything would be okay. They just went to work and did what they needed to do in order to raise a family, keep us clothed and fed. We were very conventional people. *But I was impacted by this sense of anger, that sense of having something taken away from me.*

I'm sure the roots of my shoplifting problem came when I was little, before the move. The move just exacerbated it. There's little question in my mind that if we hadn't moved, I would have continued shoplifting even back in the old home ground. But my shoplifting problem blossomed after I got my drivers license because the next memories I have of stealing anything were in high school. I still can't believe how brazen I was. We had two stores side by side, a grocery store and a store like K-Mart. There was no kind of security at that point--it was the mid '60's. I remember going from the grocery store pretending I had a grocery bag full of stuff when, in fact, it was an empty bag. I'd go to the record department and take albums. Now, that's no small feat; that's hard to do. You've got to be motivated to do that. And I was motivated. I was motivated to the point that I couldn't believe I was doing it. I don't recall how premeditated it was but it just felt miraculous I was able to get away with it.

One album I clearly remember shoplifting was George Harrison's "All Things Must Pass." I was in college at that point. There was nothing symbolic about the album or the title as far as I know. But there was the sense of having to be "on the cutting edge," the sense of having to get the latest thing. My fear of not having those items, feeling "left out," was intense. It had nothing to do with trying to impress anybody, friends. It had more to do with my sense of well-being.

C.A.S.A. helped me get in touch with the sense of ambivalence that comes with the shoplifting. For example, on the one hand, you go into the store and take these record albums, on the other hand, God, what happens if you're found out? What if people actually see these items? Or the wrong people see these items? Parents, brother. How in the world do you explain how you got it, if you're asked? In many ways there was an enabling process that was going on where certain people would see these items and not ask. It amazed me because I had very little income of my own.

The next step up was when I went to college and I went into a sporting goods store and took a pair of gloves. I got caught. The automatic idea was let's go and steal some. The truth of the matter was I didn't plan that out either, I must've been depressed, I just didn't think. I was bored one evening, went to a store, and all the sudden there they were. It was like a light bulb went off. *I'd get a big rush right before and I'd say about five or ten minutes afterwards and a sense of disbelief, kind of numb feeling after that. It also helped distract me from other issues, problems and feelings.* I was so naive, they had the big white tag or sensor thing on them and I didn't have a clue what it was, so I walked out and the electronic gate went off. This was the early '70's. I was apprehended and went through the student union who got me a lawyer and I was put under advisement, not even a real probation. *I didn't tell anyone about the arrest because secrecy was very big.*

I stopped stealing. I'm sure everything was fine for a very brief time after I got caught and did the dance of remorse. That lasted for a very brief period of time. Then, after a while, I started to steal again more regularly, lots of books. That was the pattern. *After you've gotten used to the idea of having your needs met without having to pay a price for it, the idea of having to pay for things--buy things--made me feel angry, made me feel cheated.* So there was a lot of anger involved in all of this and I didn't have many outlets for anger. I didn't realize I was angry. Even if I had, I don't think I would have had many outlets to appropriately vent.

56

I always felt--and this started even before high school--I was on the outside looking in. If there was an A list and a B list socially, I always felt I was on the B list though I was smart enough and aware enough to be on the A list. I never quite understood it. I felt like there was this big instruction book on life and I got one with a couple of chapters missing, or the ink smudged. I felt confused, angry, always because I had this sense that it wasn't that difficult for others. So there's no question I was playing that out.

My father died around the point I got out of college. *(There was a noticeable pause and void here. No emotion, no details.-Ed.)*

I went overseas and got caught twice. The first time was a very serious situation I was actually arrested shoplifting a record album but basically got off with another slap on the wrist. The second time was at a local store and, boy, was the guy pissed. He was very, very angry. He did me a favor: he said "Just cut it out!" He was more smart than angry. He was the only one in my life, up to that point, that dealt with it properly.

I did cut it out for a very long time, well, I shoplifted about once a month for about three years. I was busy working and somehow my mind was focused elsewhere. But then, through the '80's, it just started spiraling--a lot of cassettes at that point. I think it was a feeling I didn't have any roots and not being satisfied with my own life.

In the months since I started my personal growth and joined C.A.S.A., I've learned one thing that does help is a clear sense of self satisfaction. *These days part of this comes from lowering my sights about what being happy means.* Part of it is to realize some kind of balance like in the old Rolling Stones song, "You Can't Always Get What You Want" but if you try, then you get what you need. *It's possible to live without certain things, be they material or emotional.* Oddly

57

enough, if you tell yourself you're going to live without, you'll probably acquire the very same things you would have gotten otherwise. You just don't take as many chances. The need isn't as strong.

I know it's an addictive-compulsive behavior; part of it is just an instinctive feeling. Also, it's instinct based on a reaction to medication I've recently started. I've recently gone on Zoloft, an antidepressant, and I've noticed I'm much calmer, less prone to anger. I used to be very angry and I'm probably still angry but I feel a little less on edge, a little more willing to take a deep breath, relax. Things don't feel as acute as they did before. Whereas, beforehand, if I were going to shoplift, I'd have this feeling of how devoid my life was without all these various and sundry items. I'd have these thoughts about needing to get them and planning to take them. There's a lot less of that now.

I'd love to say I hit a bottom with my shoplifting but I'm afraid to because I've been there before and I realize just when I think I've gotten there, I haven't. When I was caught eight months ago--just before coming to C.A.S.A.--it was the third time I was caught since my marriage to my wife. There's no question about the pain I've inflicted on her life, our life. She could've walked. Maybe she should have. That's not for me to answer. But she didn't. She stood by my side, despite the fact that she doesn't quite understand my behavior. She's been quietly supportive, quietly helpful, she is reassured by the fact that I've gotten help both from C.A.S.A. and through counseling and medication. She's let go a little bit, too. *Before, she would take on part of the responsibility for my behavior. She doesn't do that anymore. She realizes it's my problem.* There was a guilt feeling she had within herself and I'm not sure how much I contributed to that, whether I made her feel that way as a way to deflect from my own sense of responsibility.

There's one thing I always do when I go to a C.A.S.A. meeting, and I haven't shared this with anybody. I found this little thing purely by accident. The first time I went to the meeting, I took a little nature break from the group and went into the men's room. I realized as soon as I walked into the men's room that the cinder blocks in that room resembled the last jail cell I was in. The only things in that cell were the beige cinder blocks, a mat on the floor and the basin and the toilet. Very stark, very cold. It might have been beige and it might have been silver but it was black and white to me. *And it was crystal clear--there was no denying: I was at a crossroads. And I'm still at a crossroads everyday.* So, every time I go to C.A.S.A. I go into that bathroom to remind myself of the choices that reflects.

I also realize I haven't tried to quit shoplifting cold turkey. I haven't been putting that kind of pressure on myself, like in the past. That's probably one reason I renewed the behavior. What I've been trying to do is be aware of my feelings, to give myself permission to purchase items, not necessarily in a wild, crazy, or irresponsible way--and thank God I can afford some of these things.

But I've also been trying to replace feelings of anxiety by looking for alternatives, looking for opportunities to have those needs met by alternate means. Before I would steal a video; now, I check it out of a library or rent it. Books: same thing. I try to tell myself, "No," and then feel the feelings and just relax with them. I do a lot of self talk, a lot of internal dialogue, a lot of permission to feel rather than talk myself out of feeling crummy, I acknowledge those feelings. I talk with my wife about them.

It's not always easy, and this may be where the Zoloft kicks in, where its usefulness is showing itself. I have to admit, when I met the psychiatrist to be evaluated, there was no question in his mind that this would be a helpful thing. But I was the king of skeptics, because there's something about being in the middle of an obsessive-compulsive situation; there's a lot of denial and it's hard to see yourself as governed, as anything other than a victim. I'm not sure I want to be a victim. I don't think that's helpful but there's also no question that cutting back or stopping the stealing completely has more to do with taking a deep breath and telling myself: "*Life is safe without the behavior.*"

In many ways stealing was a lifeline only because I viewed it as such. I probably will always view it as such every day of my life and that's the backdrop. That's why I have to take one day at a time to remind myself: "*It's not that important, you're giving it too much power.*" Then I have to give myself more credit and more power and remember the old truism "You can't have everything you want. Where would you put it?" Believe me, I can't speak for anybody else. But I can tell you that when the feelings are acute, you cannot steal enough, you cannot have enough. You become Mr. Materialism. After a while, it's like someone who likes steak--you can have steak four times a day but you're gonna get sick of it, both emotionally and physically, you're gonna get sick. *It's the same thing with shoplifting: there's a sickness there. There's that element of "appetite" that's involved with it and it's important to recognize this and to rise above it.*

I've been thankful to find C.A.S.A. and was amazed at how easy the group is. I had an opportunity to go a year or two before. I had a lot of resistance due to the fear of exposing myself, fear of admitting I had a problem. I guess I was afraid of the unknown, not knowing what kind of response I would get. There was also the fear of actually doing something to address the problem. So, when I did go, there was a refreshing feeling--and it was a little confusing--about just how relatively easy it was compared to my expectations. That doesn't mean it was easy. The first few weeks were very emotional for me. It felt very much like finally there was an opportunity to speak about this and only about this, to focus in on the problem and the feelings, I learned a lot about this through others' experiences and feelings, what some of the traps were.

If I have any criticisms about C.A.S.A. it has to do with whether or not we're too forgiving of the behavior or whether we do enough prevention within ourselves. It comes and goes. We're all guilty of it, including myself: being afraid of making a person who is in the midst of some bad behavior feel bad. Believe me, no one wants to feel bad and no one wants to feel superior but one thing that I've been pushing is to ask each person what they did and what they stole--not so much as what they did, I'm not trying to get better at it--but I want to put myself in that position to see how I would feel if I were in that position, so I could avoid those behaviors. Because without changing my behavior, I'm going to continue doing what I'm going to do.

To me, the only question at this stage is what's healthiest for me. There's only one person who got me into this problem and there's only one person who will get me out of the problem. My spirituality helps. It gives me a little more focus, a little more balance and it does tend to put things more in perspective in terms of what is important, what's not important. I mean, a book here or a cassette there is not going to make or break me if I were to take it or even if I wasn't going to take it.

If I were not going to buy it and I were to face the question–"Can I live without it?"–that, in effect, is the hardest question of all, in terms of the shoplifting. We have two issues here: one, is the actual behavior of stealing, of taking something that doesn't belong to you; the other issue is the anger or the void that may be there if the item in question is not in my life. So I ask myself: What's the big deal? Why is this item so important? What does it represent? Can I get it by any other means? Can I live without it if that's what's in the cards?

There are other issues, too, like fitting in with certain

crowds, having life go easier. With shoplifting, it seems there's an opportunity to have your needs met without having to sweat. Of course, that's not true, but emotionally, it seems to be true at that moment that it's easier to do that, that there's less of a loss, it's just not that hard, not that hard to do.

Today, I'm working toward resolving these issues. I don't believe they will ever fully be resolved. I think I'm setting myself up for failure if I think that one day those feelings are going to be gone. I'm much better at coping with them now, I'm better at recognizing the balance in my life and lowering the volume. But I think there will always be issues and I always have to be on my guard.

It's good to have C.A.S.A. and the support of my family. My mother found out four years ago when I was caught while visiting her out of state and she was shocked. *That was the most humiliating experience in my life.* I also always have to remember when I'm dealing with that kind of situation to think of my wife's reaction, which is hearing the phone call and feeling completely out of control and being at a crossroads as to how she should react to it. *Because in the end it's not her problem, it's my problem. And I'm putting her in that position, a crying position, and she doesn't deserve it. I don't deserve it.*

She's still learning how to trust me. I'd say it's a healthy 50-50 trust. She trusts me a little more because she sees I'm doing all kinds of things to try to mitigate the problem but she shouldn't trust me anymore than I'm willing to trust myself. I haven't earned it--I'm not talking about guilt or any kind of value judgment. I'm just talking on a very basic level. It's an old behavior and can she trust me not to do it again? No, I haven't earned that. She'd be unrealistic if suddenly she were to wake up tomorrow morning and say "I've forgotten about it." *There's no difference between this and being an alcoholic.*

Insights

Rick had a tremendous amount of insight into his shoplifting from the very start of his attending C.A.S.A. He had been in therapy and, obviously, had done a lot of self-analysis. Many people come to C.A.S.A. utterly clueless, unconscious about why they started shoplifting and what they get out of it. A common phrase is: "I don't know why I do it. I don't need the stuff I shoplift but I can't stop it and it's going to land me in jail." Yet, Rick also admitted he was out of control. What he apparently needed was a group like C.A.S.A. where he could talk to and listen to others like himself. He got another counseling referral which seemed to help and, part of the missing link may also have been the antidepressant medication. He likely realized many people attending C.A.S.A. have been on medication and, perhaps, that opened his mind to this more.

Rick echoed common, powerful themes in his life which I and most C.A.S.A. members could relate to: being denied expression of feelings as a child; being molded into "a good boy" with no tolerance for rebellion; feeling inadequate compared to others; being brought up with a survival mentality; being uprooted or suffering a loss early on; and just trying to fit in and be accepted.

There is a theory that children often take on the beliefs and patterns of their parents even when they are aware of them and don't want to. It's possible Rick took on a lot of the repressed or suppressed feelings (anger, sadness, fear) that his parents had to stuff in order to survive their Holocaust ordeals--both during the war and after. Rick spoke of being uprooted, as were his parents. He may have felt guilty even to ask for anything or have any complaints, given what his parents had been through. Even his dilemma of feeling like he didn't fit in socially growing up paled in comparison to what his folks must have felt. His parents, themselves, may have suffered what is called "survivors' guilt." Rick, too, may have taken on some of this.

Action Steps Toward Change

*Regular attendance at C.A.S.A. meetings
*Continued counseling
*Openness to medication
*Self-talk
*Practice of gratitude
*Forgiveness of self (and others)
*Focus on solutions, stay out of victim mode
*Willingness to delay gratification
*Expanding spirituality
*Willingness to feel his feelings, not overly intellectualize
*Commitment to greater intimacy with wife

Danger Signs for Relapse

*Stopping coming to C.A.S.A. meetings (overconfidence that he has "beat" shoplifting)
*Sitting on anger instead of expressing it directly when somebody angers him
*Return to over intellectualization instead of keeping centered, breathing and feeling
*Return to focus on competitiveness or comparisons
*Significant loss or change in his life

What parts of Rick's story did you most relate to or were most informative?

Sandra's and Her Husband Tom's Stories

Sandra is a 55 year old homemaker, wife, mother and grandmother. She lives in a rural suburb and is married to Tom, a retired auto engineer. Her 31 year old daughter recently died suddenly from a variety of health issues. She is strong though childlike and emotional at times. Tom is loyal and committed but frustrated with her shoplifting and other habits and ways. Sandra has been attending C.A.S.A. for 8 years and Tom attends with her occasionally for support.

I was adopted when I was five. As a child I didn't know where I belonged. I didn't find that out until I was pretty much an adult. The first time I ever stole anything I was seven or eight years old. I stole a candy bar. I stole it for a girl who I wanted to be my friend. I got caught. It was from a little Mom and Pop store on my way to school. My parents were called but I don't remember if I was punished. *Things were always very emotional.*

There was no stealing until high school except for one major incident. When I was 12 years old I was molested. I was abducted from my parents' house and before I was returned, I took twenty dollars from the guy. It was probably the twenty dollars he was going to pay the taxi to return me. I had no clear recollection of being molested. The memories only came back much later when I was married. Money became an issue for me because I never even got to keep the money, the twenty dollars. I had hid the money in my underwear and my Mom found it in the bathroom. I denied it was mine. Nothing was said about it and I never said anything to her about the incident. I just blocked it out of my mind.

I stole again in my teen years. Money was the big thing. That twenty dollars must have triggered something in me because I was still twelve when my Mom went to a graduation party with me. It was a godchild and I had gone through some ladies' purses and took some money out of them. I didn't take much so they wouldn't be able to tell it was gone. *I was probably trying to get back the twenty dollars or something symbolically.* I'm sure as a teen I took things from the drugstore. Then I remember stealing three or four aprons, fancy aprons. *That was really dumb because I didn't even like aprons.* I got caught and I stopped for a while. I don't remember my parents being called. I was scared and stopped for a long time.

I got married around the age of 22. I started shoplifting things like spices, small things, expensive. I was on a budget, twenty-five dollars a week to spend on food. *I found I just couldn't stretch it.* It was just a few spices. Then I found that it was a little bit more, a package of ham. *It started to be like a rush, something that was a secret, my secret.* My husband never suspected anything.

I was also having flashbacks of being molested almost immediately after getting married when there was sexual activity. I had a difficult time, not wanting to touch my husband. I was feeling a lot of anxiety and shame. I figured it was my fault because I had let this man molest me, I'd let him in. I didn't really let him in but my parents were renting this flat upstairs. He came to the door and asked about the flat for rent. I told him my parents weren't home. He had his foot in the door. That was my first mistake, telling him my parents weren't home. Then he came in. I don't remember what happened there but there was another time where he took me to his apartment. I couldn't tell my parents because I knew they would beat me. *So I learned how to keep secrets.*

Money was like a power thing in my marriage and the money and stealing went hand in hand. It got to be more and more. I don't remember when my purses began to get bigger and bigger but they gradually did. My husband, Tom, found out about my stealing in 1971, four years after we were married. There was a time when I was apprehended in a store by a guy I had graduated from college with. There was another time when I was actually arrested. I felt ashamed when my husband found out. *I knew I had a problem but I just thought I was a thief.* I didn't tell my husband the extent of my stealing. *I told him it was a one time thing.* There was even a prior arrest I kept from him. I hired my own attorney.

I didn't have any real idea why I was stealing. I stole things for my two daughters, things from the grocery store, cards-- cards were expensive. That was basically it. It ballooned later on. I think in part it was due to an arrest and fines to the court I was having to pay. *It was hard to make ends meet.* I was doing some ironing for extra money. *I remember feeling cheated and angry with the court for having to pay high fines.* I discovered a loophole where I could return merchandise without a receipt and get money back. Then I found out how I could take things from the store and bring them to the counter and get money back for them without even buying them.

During this time I was also getting involved in the flea market and resale business. I worked at a resale shop when the kids started school. At the flea market, I was mostly buying things from the catalogues and from garage sales, buying cheap and selling reasonable. It really didn't end up being worth it because of the expenses. *I must have had some need to collect or hoard things because my basement has been filled with boxes of knickknacks for years.* My husband hates it and I've been working gradually on getting rid of the stuff but it's hard to let go. I kept shoplifting along the way as well.

I was arrested a few more times and each time I felt more and more ashamed and lost. Everybody in my family knew but nobody really understood why I was stealing. It was almost always unplanned and it was small things that I could've paid for. I began seeing a psychiatrist and was diagnosed as bipolar, manic-depressive. Eventually, I was put on anti-depressant and anti-anxiety medications.

After my arrest in 1995, I found out about C.A.S.A. I remember looking forward to coming to my first meeting. It felt hopeful to know there were other people like me who had a problem with stealing. In the years since I've been coming to the group, I've seen a lot of changes in myself. I feel stronger. I still have issues to work on but I've come a long way. I've been through a lot, too: medication changes, marital issues, and even the recent death of my daughter who was thirty-one. Since coming to the group I have learned a lot and my stealing has decreased though I have been arrested three more times and shoplifted two other times I can recall where I wasn't arrested. *It seems I have relapsed when major issues are in my life, even when good things are happening. I shoplifted one time after my grandchild was born.*

My husband has been a source of support in some ways but we still have our problems. He has taken me to most of the weekly C.A.S.A. meetings over the last few years. Sometimes I drive myself. *He tries to understand and has learned a lot from sitting in on meetings but I don't feel he trusts me still.* He also has been helpful by doing the shopping for me or going to the store with me. He still pressures me to get rid of the stuff in the basement, though. I tell him I'm trying. *He doesn't notice the things I have done, the progress I have made.*

Tom speaks:
It has been a very challenging time for me as the husband of a shoplifter. We're just very different. I suppose I had my phase of life a long time ago where I wasn't completely honest but I grew out of it. I still don't understand her behavior fully but I have learned a lot from the group and see how shoplifting has its addictive aspects.

I think Sandra and I are different people. I feel if you've got an issue you bring it out in the open, deal with it and move on. She talks about still having issues. It's never-ending. I don't even know what those are unless it's the same old thing. I don't know if there's still some secret she's keeping. I've accepted just about everything about her. I can't believe there's anything that terrible that she's ever done--aside from murdering someone--which I couldn't deal with. I told her when I married her that I took marriage vows--to stay by her side for better or for worse. I believe in those vows. There aren't many men who would've stuck by her side after all we've been through. It's been hard.

One of the hardest things has been that I had hoped, after retiring several years ago, that we could have our freedom more, travel around the world. But I'm scared. Even when I'm by her side, she might shoplift. I don't want to risk that happening in another country. You don't know what the punishment is. You hear horror stories. I don't want to wind up in a world of shit, something we can't get out of.

I also feel frustrated that she doesn't get rid of the stuff in the basement which finds its way upstairs at times. I don't like clutter. I like to be able to walk around my own house and find a place to sit, to eat, to put something down. We've been through a lot together, though, and I don't plan on leaving. You hear a lot of people complain and think the grass is greener on the other side but it usually isn't. I try to appreciate what we do have and what matters in life.

Insights

Sandra experienced a lot of change and loss from an early age. She talked of being adopted at the age of five and, shortly after, of stealing candy to get a girl to like her. She probably felt there was something wrong with her and that's why she was put up for adoption.

The triggering event of her molestation at age 12 compounded feelings of shame and guilt and low self-esteem. Her innocence was stolen from her and she tried to steal $20 from her abuser and she wasn't even allowed to keep that. Thus, the rest of her life seems to be a recurring attempt to steal back something which was taken from her. The challenges in her marriage, both financially and intimately, created stress and conflict and, unfortunately, she never felt safe to address and resolve them.

Action Steps Toward Recovery

*Continued and consistent attendance/participation at C.A.S.A. meetings

*Continued therapy and/or psychiatric assistance

*Gradual increase in assertiveness skills (especially in her marriage

*Increase in humility and ability to ask for familial and social support

Danger Signs for Relapse

*Medication imbalance can trigger depression or mania

*Anger toward husband over control or mistrust issues

*Grief pains over recent loss of daughter

*Recurring memories of abuse

*Recurring feelings that she is a little girl with no mature coping skills

---

What parts of Sandra's or Tom's stories did you most relate to?

Part Two

Things to Consider

The Top Ten Reasons People Shoplift*

1. Grief and Loss, To Fill the Void

2. Anger/Feeling Life is Unfair, To Get Back/Make Life Right

3. Depression, To Get a Lift

4. Anxiety, To Comfort

5. Acceptance/Competition, To Fit in

6. Power/Control, To Counteract Feeling Lost/Powerless

7. Boredom/Excitement, To Live on the Edge

8. Shame/Low self-esteem, To Distract, Be Good at Something

9. Entitlement/Reward, To Compensate for Over-giving

10. Rebellion/Initiation, To Break into Own Identity

Each of these reasons were touched upon in the various stories recounted in Part One of this book and will not be elaborated upon here. You may wish to relate each reason back to part of a particular person's story.

Comparison between Kleptomania
and
Addictive-Compulsive Stealing/Shoplifting

Kleptomania (DSM IV Rev.)	Addictive-Compulsive Stealing
*Recurrent failure to resist *impulses* to steal objects *not needed* for personal use/monetary value/no premeditation	*Recurrent failure to resist *addictive compulsive* urges to steal objects which *are used*/some premeditation
*Increasing sense of tension *just before* committing the theft	*Generally, *already ever-present tension*
*Pleasure or relief *at the time of theft or *during* the theft	*Generally, pleasure or relief *shortly after* committing the theft
*The stealing is *not* committed to express anger of vengeance	*Generally, the stealing *is* a means of acting out anger or to make life fair
*The stealing is not due to Conduct Antisocial Personality Disorder	*Same. Generally, most people are honest and law-abiding

Kleptomania or Shoplifting Addiction?

As stated previously, kleptomania is a relatively rare condition. Dr. Marcus Goldman, in <u>Kleptomania</u>, states it may affect 6 out of 1000 people. Peter Berlin of Shoplifters Alternative asserts 1 out of 11 people shoplift and more than half of those become addicted to shoplifting at some stage. According to Dr. Goldman, 80% of kleptomaniacs are women, the average age of onset is 20. Shoplifters Alternative statistics state men and women shoplift equally.

Kleptomania is an impulse control disorder. What we see in our group is stealing--and shoplifting in particular--as more of an addictive-compulsive disorder.

What is the difference between an impulsive act and an addictive-compulsive act? The answer is *timing.* Addictions start as impulsive acts. The first few times I shoplifted, they were impulsive, spontaneous, unplanned acts. I developed an immediate urge to steal, did it, and it registered a desirable feeling: relief, a rush, calmness, power. Over time, though, I'd find myself obsessively thinking about stealing again. Often I'd engage in some sort of internal struggle not to do it; some time would elapse and some internal debate normally occurred. Then, at some point, the urge was so strong or the desire so tempting, I'd give in to the thoughts and feelings and shoplift.

Unlike the classic kleptomaniac who may be in a store, someone's home, or an office and feel a sudden and unplanned impulse to take something, I knew what I was doing. I consciously went to stores to get my fix. I didn't always know what I would shoplift but, generally, I had some idea. Sometimes I knew exactly what I would shoplift. *I felt compelled to get something for nothing.*

The classic kleptomaniac steals things when he/she begins to feel anxious. This person has discovered, over time, that the stealing creates an adrenaline rush which counteracts the anxiety. If kleptomaniacs have anxiety as their underpinnings, addictive-compulsive shoplifters steal more as a result of depression and anger.

Most of C.A.S.A.'s members first come to the group depressed or angry. They've shoplifted as a way to cope with these feelings, numb the feelings, or get a high to transcend these feelings in the same way a drug addict takes a drug. In addition, the desired feeling for most shoplifting addicts rarely hits at the exact time of the theft like for the kleptomaniac. It wasn't until I'd leave the store, get into my car, or got home that I'd fully feel the high. I'd feel a calmness or focus as I prepared to steal, a bit of a tingle while in the act of stealing, but I usually kept my feelings under control until I got out of the store. Then I felt a unique mix of relief, satisfaction, a buzz, nervousness or disbelief. After some short period, the guilt and depression would arise and I felt a crash or a letdown.

The classic kleptomaniac--in part due to the impulsive nature of the stealing--typically does not use or need the objects stolen and often discards or hoards them. Kleptomaniacs tend to steal things they can't use, like shoes or clothing that don't fit or multiple same items, like hundreds of pens. Similar to shoplifting addicts, kleptomaniacs steal for the feeling created by the stealing--for example, peace from anxiety--rather than for the value of the item or the item itself.

I'll admit, there have been times when I shoplifted things I didn't use but at the time of the theft I always intended using them. I shoplifted mostly music cassettes, books, food, toiletries, and knickknacks. I didn't tend to hoard but did, at times "collect." As with my early fascination with comic books, I kept a cassette tape collection on the top shelf of my clothes closet which resembled a shrine to my shoplifting.

I had underlying issues of anger and feelings that I had been cheated in life or that life was unfair. *The accumulation of objects made me feel I was getting something for nothing and tipping the scales of fairness back in balance.* Some may call this simple greed.

I look at greed as the feeling that there is never enough (which I had) but also including a disregard for the needs of others. This results in trying to keep others from having something--their due--too. That wasn't my concern. I wasn't trying to keep others from having any of the goods I was shoplifting, nor did I ever feel I was taking from anybody. The store was a nameless, faceless entity. The stores were the greedy ones. I was no Robin Hood stealing from the rich to give to the poor or to myself: it wasn't about money. *I wasn't so much trying to have more stuff as much as I was trying to fill this bottomless hole which represented my lack and my need to get back symbolically whatever was taken from me.*

This is not to say that the items meant nothing to me. If they didn't, I would have discarded them right after taking them. I wouldn't have felt the pang of having to give them up either as part of my recovery. *Shoplifting addiction is unique: not only did I get the high from the act of stealing but I also had these bonus items to show for it.* With alcohol, drug, food, and sex addictions, after the high there is only the memory: no material or physical token or souvenir remains.

If I were to shoplift and discard the items, it might satisfy my need for vengeance though the stores were not the source of my deepest anger. But I needed to feel like my stealing mattered. The gamble in itself–would I get away with it or not?–was the source of most of the adrenaline. The feeling the stealing brought was what I chased, but my high was intensified if I got away with something of perceived value to me. I enjoyed and benefitted from the items I shoplifted, yet they would lose their significance before long and I was on to shoplifting the next item.

Shoplifting addiction is most similar to gambling addiction. For the gambling addict, the money is the marker of the successful gamble, just as "winning" the item-- by not getting caught--is for the shoplifter. It's not about the money. It's about the feeling, the rush of living on the edge. Sure, the money is nice and, when, won, may be used. But more often it goes right back into the gamble. *It never ends. It's never enough. You keep chasing that rush, that high.*

The Case for Including Shoplifting Addiction
in the DSM-IV

Dr. Wil Cupchik argues in his book, <u>Why Honest People Shoplift And Commit Other Acts of Theft,</u> that there needs to be another recognized mental illness related to stealing besides kleptomania. Dr. Cupchik states there should be at least three categories of people who steal: the typical theft offender, the atypical theft offender and the mixed typical/atypical theft offender. Kleptomaniacs would fall under atypical theft offenders. Common thieves or drug addicts who steal and boost to get their fix would be more typical theft offenders. Addictive-compulsive shoplifters may fall under atypical or mixed categories. Typical theft offenders steal primarily out of need, greed, as a profession, or due to lack of conscience or morals. Atypical theft offenders are otherwise honest and law-abiding and steal in response to underlying emotional issues or conflicts. Mixed typical/atypical theft offenders may have characteristics of both.

I push things further by viewing stealing, particularly shoplifting, as a potentially addictive-compulsive behavior for which a recovery program must be a vital part of the treatment. Like gambling addiction, shoplifting addiction is characterized by a repetitive behavior--despite negative consequences--which becomes difficult to control and has common "withdrawal" symptoms such as preoccupation, anxiety, depression, and edginess.

Most people shoplift out of anger, yet, it is not a given that if you resolve the anger issues--which can take years--you stop shoplifting forever. My experience has been that resolving anger issues will decrease shoplifting but won't necessarily end it. I've witnessed this among most others as well. Once addicted, one develops an automatic or habitual response to certain thoughts, feelings, events, or situations. As daily frustrations occur, most remain vulnerable to being triggered to relapse. It takes ongoing cognitive-behavioral fine tuning to stop the behavior.

The reverse is also true. The shoplifting has to lessen or cease in order for one to begin addressing the sources of the behavior and return to saner thinking. Recovery groups have been highly effective in providing the necessary support to curtail or stop the behavior first, long enough to minimize the chaos of life, provide some manageability, so the underlying issues can be pinpointed and eventually resolved. Recovery provides an ongoing context for growth, re-building of self-esteem, awareness of self-defeating patterns, and reduction of relapses.

We need more groups where people can receive the help they need and then give it back to others. Unfortunately, the shame associated with shoplifting is so monumental that this may be many years away.

Some Statistics from C.A.S.A.

My best estimates of some key statistics of the 700 persons who have attended C.A.S.A. in Detroit from 12/92-6/03.

---

*65% women
*35% men
*60% directly court-ordered
*30% begin after arrest but before being court-ordered
*10% "voluntary" (came on their own)
*70% have been previously arrested
*25% first arrest
*5% never been arrested
*70% report 1st theft as a child
*20% report 1st theft as a teen
*10% report 1st theft as an adult
*25% report shoplifting nearly daily
*40% report shoplifting at least 1x/week
*20% report shoplifting at least 1x/month
*10% report shoplifting around 1x/year
*5% report shoplifting one time
*30% report other addictions (food, alcohol/drugs, gambling)
*50% co-dependent
*70% report severe shame from shoplifting
*70% report suffering from depression and/or anxiety
*30% report currently seeing a counselor
*50% report have seen a counselor at some time
*35% report taking some form of psychiatric medication
*25% attend C.A.S.A. over 1 year (shoplifting virtually stops)
*50% attend C.A.S.A. for 6 mos-1year (shoplifting greatly reduced)
*20% attend C.A.S.A. for less than 6 mos (shoplifting lessens)
*5% attend C.A.S.A. one time and never return

The Seven Different Types of Shoplifters

1. *The Professionals*
2. *The Drug and Gambling Addicts*
3. *The Impoverished*
4. *The Thrill Seekers*
5. *The Absent-Minded*
6. *The Kleptomaniacs*
7. *The Addictive Compulsive*

1. The"Professionals"

(Those who steal for profit/greed/lifestyle/job)

I estimate this group accounts for 2% of those who shoplift but they make a huge dent in losses to stores because when they hit, they hit hard. I estimate professionals account for 10% of shoplifting losses.

Who is the professional shoplifter?:

*Look for expensive or "high end" items stolen

*Look for multiple items stolen at a time

*Look for accomplices (part of a shoplifting "ring")

*May have few or no prior arrests (plots thefts well)

*May have several or many arrests (due to frequency of thefts. Professionals don't stop after arrests, they chalk it up to a cost of doing business)

*May have a criminal record of other crimes of dishonesty (larcenies, burglaries, fraud) from stores, offices, homes

*May have articles to help circumvent security systems (scissors, overcoats, expandable clothing, etc.)

*Likely to resist arrest or attempt to flee store premises

*Does not appear emotional or remorseful (cool and calm)

*Does not answer questions, gives little information about self

*Usually unmarried (to avoid suspicion about lifestyle)
*Usually under-employed as shoplifting may be a full-time job
*May be male or female
*May also be drug-addicted or gambling addict

NOTE: The "professional" shoplifter is not ideally suited for C.A.S.A. or therapy. This individual may have a personality disorder that is difficult to treat, little conscience, and a deeply ingrained sense of materialism. C.A.S.A. has seen a few professionals over the years and they tend to disrupt the group with their lack of remorse, insight, and appreciation of the negative consequences of shoplifting. In short, they don't want to change. They tend to glorify or boast about their shoplifting. They refer to their shoplifting as a choice, not an addiction, and chalk up their arrests to their carelessness or bad luck.

----

2. The Drug and Gambling Addicts

(Those who steal to support an underlying addiction)

I estimate these shoplifters account for 2% of all shoplifters but who make a large dent in stores' losses due to the frequency of thefts and the greater expense of the items stolen. These addicts shoplift and sell the goods to get money for drugs, alcohol or to pay their debts or to get more money for gambling. These people will continue shoplifting after arrest if their underlying addiction is not treated.

Who is shoplifting to support an underlying addiction?:

*Look for expensive or "high-end" items stolen
*Look for prior arrests for other thefts or crimes of dishonesty
*Likely to have repeated arrests for shoplifting (not as

careful/skilled as professionals as addiction may interfere with perception and awareness of environment

*Look at person's appearance. Does he/she look sickly, agitated, unkempt, disheveled, "high" or "wired"?

*Look for drugs/drug paraphernalia at time of their arrest

*Look for signs of gambling addiction (lottery tickets, casino chips, betting slips)

*Look for substance abuse history (arrests or treatment)

*Likely to resist arrest or attempt to flee store due to fear of arrest/incarceration, addictive state

*May be under-employed, no legal means of getting money

*Does not answer questions, gives little information about self

----

NOTE: These shoplifters are not ideally suited for C.A.S.A. or for traditional individual counseling. They may need more intensive treatment until the underlying addiction is managed. Treating drug--and gambling addiction–is an urgent matter. Suicides, accidents, overdoses, and homicides are all too real consequences of these addictions. C.A.S.A. has seen many former, recovering drug addicts and alcoholics who've reported shoplifting to support their habits. Many have stated they found themselves addicted to shoplifting when they stopped using drugs and/or alcohol.

----

3. The Impoverished

(Those who steal out of real or perceived economic need)

I estimate that 5% of shoplifters fall into this category. There is never an excuse for shoplifting--even if one is suffering hard times. Yet, this group shoplifts out of survival instinct to help themselves, their families or others. This figure fluctuates with unemployment rates, the state of the economy.

Who is shoplifting out of perceived economic need/survival?:

*Look for inexpensive items stolen

*Look for "necessity items" (food, diapers, toiletries, kids'clothes, medications, etc.)

*Look for under-employment/no job/recent lay-off

*Person usually has children

*Person is generally scared or remorseful

*Person's dress or hygiene may be poor

*May have suffered recent loss (move, divorce, death, illness)

NOTE: The impoverished person is not ideally suited for C.A.S.A. or traditional counseling as the individual may continue to feel the need to shoplift to survive. Referral to social service agencies may be best. However, C.A.S.A. or counseling may help such persons by giving them a place to vent their feelings and learn more healthy coping skills for their situations as well as more creative--and legal--ways to make ends meet.

---

4. The Thrill Seekers

(Those who steal for excitement/a dare/or peer pressure)

I estimate this group accounts for 5% of those who shoplift. This includes teens *before* they become addicted–this is the early stage. Teens may belong in other categories as well. This group includes adults who shoplift occasionally and people who have a pattern of thrill seeking behaviors–*it's about boredom/peer pressures, not anger, depression, loss, or anxiety*

Who is shoplifting as a thrill or a dare?:

*Look for many teens in this category

*Motivated by rebellion, pressure to fit in, boredom
*The shoplifting is often done in groups of young people
*Items stolen are usually inexpensive
*May engage in risky behaviors (smoking, drugs, speeding, sex)
*Likely has problems in school
*Likely impulsive, has signs of attention deficit disorder

NOTE: People become addicted to the adrenaline rush shoplifting provides. C.A.S.A. has been successful in helping them by emphasizing the negative consequences of shoplifting (arrest, lowered trust by others, lowered self-esteem) and by suggesting safer, natural, legal ways of getting thrills.

---

5. The Absent-Minded

(Those who are truly forgetful)

Accidents do happen. *Occasionally.* I estimate this group makes up about 1% of all shoplifters. Forgetfulness can result from organic conditions--like Alzheimer's, seizures, panic disorders, or in the rush of this hurried life. Most stores and courts have become skeptical about any "real" accidents in shoplifting. In most states, the crime of shoplifting occurs when the item is concealed, not when leaving the store with it.

Who may be an accidental or truly forgetful shoplifter?:

*Look for Alzheimer's symptoms, history of seizures or panic
*Look for elderly persons
*Look for most or many items paid for
*Look for lack of effort to conceal item

*Look for genuinely surprised reaction at being caught
*May be only one item stolen and nothing else purchased

NOTE: C.A.S.A. is not ideally suited for this group of people but has seen several who have been court-ordered which indicates there needs to be better screening. These folks may need counseling and increased support and assistance.

6. The Kleptomaniacs

(Those who steal impulsively for "no reason")

I estimate this group accounts for 1% of those who shoplift. Kleptomania is a rare impulse control disorder, committed mostly by women above age 20. The items stolen are usually discarded, or are not able to be used (clothes that don't fit, multiple items of the same thing).

Who is the kleptomaniac shoplifter?:

*Look for women usually above age 20
*Look for signs of tension or anxiety
*Look, generally, for inexpensive items stolen
*Look for items which the person doesn't need or can't use (shoes or clothes that don't fit, multiple same items)
*Look for items stolen near the check-out line (where anxiety may increase while waiting)
*Look for common explanations: "I don't remember taking it" or "I don't know why I took it"
*Look for multiple arrests
*Look for verification of person in therapy and/or especially on medication for anxiety or obsessive-compulsive behavior
*Look for lack of anger response to being caught

NOTE: Therapy and medication are the best treatment for kleptomania. Though we call the group C.A.S.A. to include kleptomaniacs, the group is better suited for persons who are addicted to stealing and who benefit from a recovery program. While many C.A.S.A. members have shown some signs of kleptomania--sometimes stealing things impulsively, things that were not needed, multiple items of the same kind, and things which were hoarded--most differ from kleptomaniacs due to frequent and prior compulsive feelings and planning of thefts, and significant underlying anger issues which contributed to starting and continuing the shoplifting/stealing.

C.A.S.A. has only seen a few classic kleptomaniacs and many who showed some but not all the signs of kleptomania. The group may be helpful in providing shame reduction through talking/listening to others and getting ideas for stress and anxiety reduction and coping.

----

7. The Addictive-Compulsive
(Those who act out and get hooked)
I estimate is that this group accounts for nearly 85% of all shoplifters and more than half of stores' external losses.

Who is a shoplifting addict?:

*Look for multiple arrests (often within a short period of time to suggest a lack of control over the shoplifting)

*Look for no prior arrests (may have just become addicted or just got caught for the first time)

*Rule out economic motivation (can afford what they shoplift and often have the money on them at the time of arrest)

*Items stolen are usually inexpensive

*Items stolen are to be used or given to others as gifts

*Many or most items are paid for at time of arrest

*Look for guilt, shame or remorse ("tears or fears")

*Look for fear about others finding out about arrest (secret)

*Look for offers to pay for merchandise stolen

*Look for significant personal problems or emotional stresses in life (especially losses or changes in life)

*Look for other addictions like drugs/alcohol/gambling, etc.

*Look for common traits of caretakers/co-dependents (stuffed anger, more concern about others and how they will be affected by their shoplifting arrest)

*Look for lack of insight into behavior, numbness

*May be in therapy or on medication for depression

NOTE: Therapy and C.A.S.A. are ideally suited for this group of persons. C.A.S.A. is for those who have used shoplifting or stealing as a way to cope with life's stresses, numb feelings, and provide a lift from depression. C.A.S.A. helps reduce shame and emphasizes accountability and helps people gain insight while changing their behaviors and learning how to cope with life, especially with anger and depression

---

Getting Arrested: What You Need to Know

Most people's first arrest is a shock to the system. My first experience was nothing short of terrifying and humiliating. I remember feeling as if I had shrunk into a little ball. The store manager was rough and mean. She grabbed me, yelled at me. Those few minutes of not knowing what was going to happen to me--would I go to jail, be taken in a squad car?-- were gut-wrenching. I worried I'd be taken out in handcuffs for the world to see.

Most people in C.A.S.A. have similar stories. Many felt like victims most of their lives and they tend to focus on their perceived, or actual, mistreatment by the store personnel, the police, the judge, probation officers, even their own attorneys ("He didn't have much sympathy for me," "She made a ton of money off me.") *Often, getting arrested further stokes the shoplifter's underlying anger or feelings of unfairness.* Where does the unfairness end?

Subsequent arrests and court dates elicit fear of being punished more severely for the repeated offense. I could relate to the countless stories I've heard at C.A.S.A. about the anxiety of feeling "like my life is in limbo" while waiting for the final court outcome. For many, this lasts for more than a year.

I highly recommend hiring a good attorney or, at least, asking for a court-appointed attorney. While I pled guilty both times I was arrested for shoplifting (1986 and 1990) and had no intention of fighting either case, I'm glad I had an attorney. It helped me sleep better at night, helped me be less anxious on each court date, and helped me get a decent plea bargain where I felt I received a fair consequence instead of "having the book thrown at me." The attorney in my second case presented to the judge the letter from my psychologist better than I could have done for myself.

For those who have never been arrested and those who may have gone through legal proceedings and felt like it was all a blur, the following steps usually apply in criminal offense procedures:

1. Waiting. Waiting to be formally charged after your arrest (notice usually comes by mail or phone from a police detective). This can take a week to several months as the police show the evidence to the local prosecutor who makes the decision whether there's enough evidence to prosecute.

2. Preliminary Exam. There is the preliminary exam on a felony charge or an arraignment on a misdemeanor charge. A felony is an offense punishable by more than one year in jail or prison; a misdemeanor is punishable up to one year. With shoplifting, or retail fraud as it's often called, states' laws vary. In Michigan, one can be charged as a felon on any second retail fraud offense no matter what value the item is, or on the first offense if the value of the item exceeds $1,000.00 (One Thousand Dollars). A misdemeanor charge is anything under that. Changing or switching price tags, doing false returns, and other fraud in a store may also be charged as retail fraud.

In the preliminary exam, initial witnesses are called (store security, police officer, etc.) order to testify about the details of the offense and the arrest in for a judge to determine if there is reasonable suspicion the crime was committed by the defendant. It is not a full trial and guilt beyond a reasonable doubt need not be shown.

The defendant's attorney can waive the preliminary exam or let it be held and cross-examine witnesses. In cases where witnesses fail to show or the judge determines the testimony and evidence against the defendant is nil, the charge may be dismissed after the preliminary exam. If the exam is waived or held and the judge finds there is reasonable suspicion the case is "bound over" to the circuit court for an arraignment.

3. Arraignment. In the circuit court for felonies and in the district court for misdemeanors, this is the stage of the case at which the formal charge may be read and an initial plea of guilty, not guilty, stand mute, or no contest is entered. It is also the stage at which to request a court-appointed attorney or have some time to hire one. If a guilty plea is entered at this stage, there may be immediate sentencing or, more, likely, referral to the probation department for a "pre-sentence investigation" or interview (PSI) prior to returning before the judge for sentencing.

4. Pre-Trial. The pre-trial conference is the plea bargain or motion filing stage. It usually takes place one to two months after the arraignment if a not guilty plea is entered. A guilty plea can be entered on this pretrial date and immediate sentencing or referral to probation for a PSI occurs.

5. Trial. The trial date (before a judge or a jury) is usually a month or two after the pre-trial. A guilty plea may also be entered on this date.

6. Sentencing. The sentencing date before a judge occurs after a guilty plea or a conviction at trial; sometimes there is immediate sentencing after the plea or conviction--usually with first-time offenders--but, more often, a PSI is requested. The PSI may be scheduled immediately or within a month. Formal sentencing usually happens within a month after the PSI.

7. Probation. Instead of--or in addition to--being incarcerated, most shoplifters are put on probation. This is a time period, usually six months to two years. Probation may be reporting or non-reporting to a probation officer. It may include fines and costs, community service, attendance in counseling, education groups, support groups, or other court-ordered programs, or the wearing of an electronic tether. If you violate any term of probation (new arrest, unpaid fines, no-show for appointment, etc.) you will likely extend your probation period, add additional costs or duties, and/or go to jail.

The reality is you do not feel free and your life will feel on hold. Many C.A.S.A. members have spoken of the humiliation of going to a court and risking seeing someone he or she knows. Humiliation is part of the price we pay.

Some group members tend to focus on the details of their arrest or their court proceedings or their interactions with their probation officers. They look to gain support from the group about how unfair they've been treated. We realize people need to vent about their experiences but we will also prod them to focus on the present, to owning up to their shoplifting--even if it's an addiction--which put them in this mess, and on recovery issues such as how to cope with anger. We encourage them to move on, learn from this, and how to avoid repeating the same behavior, how to recognize patterns of victimization.

I know how hard it is to feel your life is in limbo. If you are reading this and are currently waiting for your court proceedings--or your probation--to end, I just want to remind you: "This, too, shall pass." It will end. Keep your focus, do what you need to do: show up for court/probation, listen to your attorney. Remember that the real issue is what are you going to do with your life to make sure you change it? If you have severe anxiety, this will be difficult. But this *is* your chance to employ new ways of coping with that anxiety: breathing, prayer, meditation, exercise, a hobby, sharing with someone you trust. You are on the path toward recovery.

8. *Expungement.* In most states, misdemeanors and sometimes felonies, can be removed from your criminal record after some years have passed–usually five–without further incident. However, law enforcement will always retain some back-up record of its having been there. I had my misdemeanor retail fraud conviction from 1990 removed in 1996.

How To Avoid Stores

Even after being arrested, many shoplifters are resistant to avoiding stores. Many act as if it is utterly impossible, that they would not be able to survive without going to stores. Many are unwilling to make such sacrifices at all, even in early recovery. Others fear they will have to ask for help from others–which is part of recovery. Others are not willing to admit they cannot go about life "normally" and go in and out of stores as they please like others who do not have a shopping or shoplifting problem.

To this dilemma, I say: "Hello! Wake up!" In early recovery, at least, you need to not only take the bullet out of the gun, you need to take the gun out of your hand. Stores, for the vulnerable shoplifter, are like guns. Plain and simple. There's an old saying: *"If you keep going into the barbershop, eventually you're going to get your hair cut."*

Also, consider the following:

*A recovering alcoholic avoids bars, liquor stores, other alcoholics
*A recovering drug addict avoids other narcotics addicts, places where drugs are sold/used
*A recovering gambling addict avoids casinos, party stores where lottery tickets are sold, sporting events if sports betting has been a problem
*A recovering food addict avoids places where certain foods are too tempting
*A recovering sex addict avoids pornography, sex shops, places where prostitutes roam.
*A recovering shopping addict avoids stores and other triggers

Are you serious about recovery and willing to go to any length to get it? People are in denial about how powerless they are over their shoplifting addiction. They think they can resist temptation. In fact, addicts want to convince themselves that they are under control by demonstrating how they can say "no" and exercise some willpower in certain situations.

You can play this game but don't expect any real change. You might go to the store early in your recovery and not shoplift–you may even have no urge to do so--but it is just a matter of time before you will.

For most people, shopping is a necessity and it is hard to avoid stores altogether. But recovery is a matter of creating new choices, new coping skills, a new lifestyle. In my case I was fortunate because I was single and able to avoid stores a lot because I didn't have to shop for anyone but myself. Also, I never was very big into shopping or browsing or spending/buying as a form of hobby or fulfillment. Still, it was an adjustment. I've known *shopaholics* who have been able to stay out of stores and fill up their lives with new things to do.

Recovery is tough for all addicts because eventually we will be exposed to temptations to learn how to set boundaries:
*Shopping addicts need to learn how to go shopping at times
*Food addicts need to eat
*Alcoholics will find themselves around alcohol at times
*Sex addicts will want to have sex eventually
*Co-dependents will want to help others
*Shoplifting addicts will need to go to stores at some point

We must find new ways to spend our time, especially when bored, angry, lonely, empty or depressed--any of those warning signs which can lead to a relapse. I occupied myself by spending time at support groups, walking, reading. When I shopped--for clothes, books, food--I made sure I was in a relatively centered state of being. Generally, I said a prayer or affirmation before going into the store: "Just go in and get what you need." "Don't browse. You're doing well." I carried a smooth stone in my pocket. Dave, a long-time C.A.S.A. member, came up with the idea of giving stones out to each member. The stone reminds me of the group, of our power, and it keeps my hands from taking.

Go shopping with others if that is likely to prevent you from shoplifting. If this is too tempting, ask others to shop for you. This may be a stretch but will nurture growth in your ability to ask for help from others, a common challenge among most C.A.S.A. members.

I also budgeted my money. I used my credit card a lot more in recovery and, for a brief period, I overspent. It is easy to go from being a shoplifting addict to being a shopping addict in a heartbeat. If your budget is a concern and you are prone to scarcity thinking, be creative and find ways to recycle or make items you need or gifts for others. Go bargain hunting, shop at flea markets, resale shops, garage sales or other places where you are less likely to steal. Most shoplifting addicts find it more tempting to steal from large stores than small stores. Large stores may have more security but they are more "faceless" and impersonal than small stores.

Someone to Talk To

All addictions thrive on shame and secrecy. Therefore, it is imperative you find at least one trustworthy person you can share your story with. Step 5 of the 12 steps states the importance of this. I first shared my shoplifting secret with my girlfriend, Juniper. She then shared some secret addictive behavior of hers with me. So, trusting her led to her trusting me. That was a positive thing. She was in therapy and encouraged me to get help. She told me she suspected I was stealing because of the gifts I'd give her and others. I wasn't as secretive or slick as I thought. *People in your life already know or have some idea you have stolen. We're only as sick as our secrets.*

However, telling another person about your secretive behavior should be done with the intention to get support to help stop the behavior. When I first told Juniper, I didn't have an intention to stop shoplifting. It was a step in the right direction but what I wanted was to see if she would accept me even with this behavior. I was testing her love for me-- what I thought was "unconditional love." Find someone you can trust to tell.

So, eventually, I used this confession to alleviate my guilt and shame just enough to continue shoplifting. It wasn't her job to fix me or track my progress. But by accepting no real commitment from me to change, she enabled me to continue. I accept responsibility for my behavior but I think this is an important point in relationships. Most of us don't have the skills or the insight to challenge a loved one's behaviors in an appropriate, transforming way.

Ideally, what may have been most helpful to me would have been if she had said something like: "Terry, I'm glad you have shared this secret with me. I appreciate your trust in me. I have some things I need to share with you as well. You are not a bad person but this behavior is destructive to you and to us. I need you to commit to getting help for this immediately because our relationship cannot be healthy as long as you are doing this and I can't be in a relationship like this."

Instead, six months went by. I continued to shoplift and engaged in an affair. I hit a bottom which may have been avoided. I was on a downward spiral, suicide was the next step.

Fortunately, I reached out for help before it was too late. A week later I was in therapy. People need to feel safe and not judged by their therapists. There are not enough therapists who understand or can treat shoplifting addiction. I've used therapy as a "confessional." I dumped my secrets, alleviated my guilt, and continued to repeat the behavior.

Recovery is an ongoing and deepening commitment to changing behavior patterns which, in turn, change you. Stopping stealing is a process which, over time, results in a stronger ability to choose and commit to life. Each day I must make a choice not to steal. Some days this is not a big deal; on others, it is extremely hard to resist returning to the old ways of trying to cope with feelings and life.

But the bottom line is this: stealing does not help me. Shoplifting doesn't solve anything and never will. "Once is too many and a thousand times is never enough."

What To Do With The Stolen Merchandise

For many members in C.A.S.A., myself included, this issue has resurfaced time and again: What do I do with the things I still have that I stole? For most, there is a very difficult decision to make. One of my therapists, Dr. Brownfain, demanded I get rid of all the things I had stolen, things laying around possibly reminding me of the past, things I continued to hoard needlessly or directly benefit from or enjoy.

I was afraid of getting rid of these things because, on some level, I was still attached to them or, at least, what they represented to me: namely, a bit of pain and victory in getting something back from life. How many of us have experienced the thrill of getting something for nothing, legitimately (or illegitimately)? Having to return a gift, prize, or reward is not an easy thing to do. *There's something primal about possession.*

Relinquishing my attachment to the items I shoplifted was part of a Step Nine, a making of amends. My experience was positive in the end. Holding onto stolen goods, in my opinion, is a form of not letting go, a form of holding onto the past. I advocate getting rid of the "tainted fruit of the bounty." But timing is key. There's that line between letting go too abruptly and dragging your feet. Many C.A.S.A. members have disagreed with me on the value and need to let go of the things.

When you feel ready to let go of the objects, I suggest you do so a little at a time. I recommend either throwing them away or donating them to a charity--and not taking the tax deduction. There were a few times when I returned an item to the store anonymously through the mail or left it at the doorstep. Once I sent a short note and some cash. It would be great to take everything back directly to the stores, apologize to a real live person, and then pay for the items or arrange some other restitution. This, however, can be dangerous and risky. You may open yourself up for arrest which won't be the best thing for your recovery and may continue your stealing due to trauma.

If you have a therapist, you may wish to explore whether the items you shoplifted had any particular symbolic value for you. I know that I shoplifted mainly cassette tapes and I feel on some level it was symbolic because my father was a pianist before he became an attorney. My happiest memories were of listening to him play. I believe he also was happiest when he was playing. Perhaps I was attempting to steal back the happiness, the memories from my childhood.

A few C.A.S.A. members have tried sneaking items back into stores by leaving them inside or on the shelf. This is risky because you can get arrested that way and the very act of being sneaky in returning an item creates a very similar experience to sneaking to steal. If you are feeling guilty, I'd suggest finding a way to make an amend that doesn't put you at risk. If you are feeling a need to punish yourself by getting caught again, don't. *You've punished yourself and others enough.* People shoplift to help cope with feelings and issues. Returning to shoplifting to beat yourself up for what you've done to your life because of shoplifting is a vicious cycle. It never ends. Turn off the ass-kicking machine.

The Dangers of Transferring Addictions

There is a tendency for an addict to stop one addiction and return to an old addiction, develop a new addiction, or cross over the line to an addiction "in progress." An example is someone who stops smoking may develop or re-activate a food addiction. When an alcoholic gives up booze, he or she may substitute caffeine. Most addicts latch onto dysfunctional, co-dependent relationships in early recovery.

When I stopped shoplifting, like layers of an onion being peeled away, my co-dependency revealed itself clearly. Three months after my father died I got involved with an emotionally and financially needy woman with three children. I was determined to save her and them. This relationship went on and off for nearly four years. While my shoplifting had ceased, my relationship became the chaotic salvation which filled my void. This is typical. Gradually, the layers of the onion peel away until you hit the core. This is the real you, the real pain, the real gold. There's nowhere else to hide. Many never get there.

Here are some of the more common addictions which recovering shoplifting addicts tend to pick up when they let go of the shoplifting and stealing:

Eating Disorders

Many shoplifters have reported eating disorders began or were exacerbated as they gave up shoplifting. There are obvious reasons for this. There's a void when the stealing stops or decreases and food is easily available to comfort the depression and anxiety. Boredom and restlessness ensue and it becomes tempting to nibble to pass the time. Eating disorders, while not illegal like shoplifting, are life-threatening and, at minimum, contribute to depression, anxiety, low self-esteem and, eventually, a likely temptation to shoplift again. It's a Catch-22.

If you know that overeating or a food addiction is a risk for you, be proactive and get the support of family and friends and possibly a family doctor, therapist or nutritionist. If it seems inevitable that you will be munching for a while, at a minimum, switch to lower calorie and healthier foods. Begin some sort of exercise program--as hard as that may be--to fill the void that is left when you stop shoplifting. Exercise, helps balance one's moods by releasing endorphins and by providing an outlet for the stress one feels in early recovery.

Warning: Even exercise can become an addiction if you overdo it. Certain people with addictive personalities don't know moderation and do everything to excess. There are no positive addictions: anything done excessively can contribute to negative consequences. If you are exercising and injuring yourself, you might not even be aware of it at first. If it's impacting your significant relationships or obligations-Stop!

Gambling Addiction

Shoplifting addicts, in my opinion, must be gamblers at heart. I never considered this at first because I've always hated gambling in its other forms--casinos, card and sports betting--because I've valued balance, stability, and hard work. But I must admit, there's a part of me that needs to live on the edge. *Shoplifting is a form of gambling.* Each time I stole from a store I was gambling that I'd get away with it. I was gambling with my freedom because if I was arrested, that might be taken away, not to mention the other consequences I risked: my relationships, my peace of mind, my future. Shoplifting is like Russian Roulette to me now. Fortunately, I choose not to play.

A gambling addiction can get activated or reactivated in a heartbeat when one stops shoplifting. You're still going to be looking for that rush, that high. Even an innocent trip to a casino can get you--especially if you win but even if you lose--and the bigger the loss, the more the tendency is for the recovering shoplifter to try to get it back by shoplifting.

I don't go to the casinos. This is not a place for a recovering person to be anyway. There's a frenetic energy there which triggers a buzz for people similar to being in a big store. There are all kinds of addicts in casinos: gambling addicts, alcoholics, drug addicts, shoplifting addicts, not to mention various criminals, drug dealers, thieves, mobsters and prostitutes. I know this sounds harsh but I'd rather be safe than sorry. The allure of winning something for nothing (or for very little) can trigger the shoplifting addict all over again.

If you feel the need to gamble or seek thrills, take up a hobby like skydiving, rock climbing or something that challenges your mind, excites you. Let the excitement of personal growth work engage you. Give it time.

Shopping Addiction

A lot of shoplifters start off on the verge of becoming or are already shopping addicts. Our society promotes shopping addiction, materialism and consumerism. How does one define shopping addiction? Some have referred to it as "compulsive buying." Dr. Donald W. Black, in an article on the subject, defines it as *"chronic, repetitive purchasing that becomes very difficult to stop and ultimately results in harmful consequences."* Such consequences can be unmanageable debts, fights with spouse or family members over expenditures, neglecting other financial, physical or emotional needs by spending money elsewhere, and avoiding issues or feelings by shopping. If a person starts out with a shopping addiction, it becomes tempting to start shoplifting as a way of budgeting money, rationalizing that one isn't buying as much or spending as much if one is stealing.

The temptation to become shopping addicts when giving up

shoplifting is strong. At first I kept out of the stores for a long time and cut down dramatically on my need to have things. I spent most of my money on therapy and personal growth related things such as weekend retreats but, at times, books, cassettes, videos, etc. I began using my credit card more often because it seemed like it hurt less than spending cash. I found myself a little over my head at times and, fortunately, realized what was happening and checked it. Later, when I began a romantic relationship, I found myself spending more on dining out, on gifts, on vacations. I, again, went over my comfortable budget and had to reign it in.

Recovery includes budgeting one's money, learning how to do without, taking a hard look at wants vs. needs, and negotiating with a partner or family members about how the money will be spent.

Some suggestions to follow:

*Commit to some time to go through the house and organize and discover what can still be used: this can be food, clothing, appliances, etc.

*Get rid of things that you no longer need or want--perhaps selling them at a flea market or garage sale or donating them to charity for a tax deduction.

*Create a budget and a means of sticking to it.

*Find a balanced, patient, and responsible way to gradually pay off debts without feeling hopeless if you don't pay them off tomorrow

*Reward yourself in modest and healthy ways with your money

*Ask for help financially from others if you need to

*Take up a hobby to fill the time and to focus your attention to give an outlet for your emotions

Gray Area Dishonest Behaviors

Gray area behaviors come up in every recovery path. Gray area behaviors are "lesser" forms of the primary addiction which compromise one's recovery and still constitute a relapse. For example, the recovering alcoholic whose primary drink was hard liquor might rationalize drinking beer, though it's obvious to others it's basically the same thing in a lesser form. At one time, he may have agreed that drinking beer was not acceptable but as his life became more manageable, he decided he can have a little. He rationalized a sip of champagne at a celebration is okay, or that it's safe to drink non-alcoholic beer, "near beer," which has one-half a percent alcohol per 12 ounces and smells and tastes similar to regular beer.

Gray area behaviors keep the denial system alive and likely contribute to full relapse. Here are other examples:

* The gambling addict no longer goes to the casinos but still bets on sports or buys lottery tickets
* The drug addict no longer uses heroin but still takes Tylenol with codeine
* The compulsive overeater switches from junk food to more nutritious food but still compulsively overeats.
* The sex addict stops seeing prostitutes, having affairs, using pornography, but becomes hooked on Internet interludes

Each person draws his or her own "line in the sand" about what recovery means and how much addictive behavior to eliminate. Ongoing counseling and/or support groups explore, challenge these gray area behaviors. As denial breaks, deeper levels of understanding develop, and behaviors naturally change for the better.

I report my gray area behaviors openly and honestly at C.A.S.A. each week. Others have shared theirs as well. We have frank discussions about whether this or that is stealing, whether it constitutes a relapse, how to avoid repeating the behaviors. We never condone gray area behaviors; rather, we emphasize the costs: guilt and anxiety over, loss of faith, full relapse, humiliation, rejection when caught. We acknowledge continuing to steal in any form is a sign of holding onto anger and fear, a refusal to let go and trust life, others, ourselves.

Recovery is about progress not perfection. It is an ongoing journey. I'm still keenly alert to opportunities to get "something for nothing" and have to watch myself daily.

Some Common Gray Area Dishonest Behaviors

Taxes

Shortly after we married, my wife and I hired a financial advisor. It was one of the best investments we've ever made, financially and psychologically. It may also help our marriage as most marriages break up over money issues. I used to be afraid to report all my true earnings to the government so they wouldn't tax me as much. You can't do this if your income is all from an employer on your W-2 form. But if you take side work and are, at least partly, self-employed this is possible. I under reported my income. But I also under reported my expenses and deductions because I was ignorant about how to claim all of these on the up and up. Our financial advisor has taught me a lot. Now I am truthful about what I make and the more money I claim, the more money I can deduct without it looking suspicious. It's a win-win and it's all above-board. What a shift. I pay my advisor from the money I save using him.

I've known a few folks who've had trouble with the IRS due to fraud on their part. It costs a lot of time, money and aggravation. People with anti-government sentiments who don't who don't want to pay all or some of their taxes may find other ways to protest that will not get them in hot water. Or hire a good financial advisor who can limit your tax liability legally. *Make a commitment to do the right thing.*

Cash Adding Mistakes

If only this happened more often! What would you do if you were given too much money back from the store clerk? The bank teller? A customer or client of yours? Anybody for that matter. Does your answer change depending on who it is that makes the mistake? If so, why? What's the difference?

Sometimes when at the bank or a store, a clerk makes a mistake and gives you back more money than you are supposed to get. This has happened to me several times and I am always alerted to it immediately because I still have the "something for nothing" bug. We talk about this kind of thing at C.A.S.A. It's odd, on some occasions I have accepted the mistaken money and on some occasions I have returned it. It's rarely been more than a buck or two. On the occasions I've chosen not to return the money, I'm usually feeling ungrounded, angry, or stressed. I get a little buzz over getting something for nothing but feel that tinge of guilt, knowing I just missed life's little opportunity to be honest "when nobody was looking."

When I chose to return money given to me in error, it usually happened very quickly, as if a higher part had taken over. While I usually felt disappointment over my lost "gain," I nevertheless felt a sense of pride and accomplishment, knowing how much I'd changed, how far I'd come.

False Returns of Merchandise

There are a number of ways in which people who shoplift or steal take back merchandise, exchanging, getting store credit, or getting cash back for merchandise one didn't even buy.

Say, I buy something, then break it or decide afterwards I don't want it. If I go back to the store and lie about this, saying it was broken when I bought it or it was a gift that wasn't wanted, this is a continuation of the addictive behavioral pattern. It is a refusal to play by the rules. There are those who routinely buy things intending only to use them for a while, then return them. This can be driven by scarcity mindedness, a need for trickery, the need to outsmart or dupe someone to get even or make yourself feel "one up." This takes a lot of time and energy and keeps life chaotic.

I used to engage in these behaviors. For instance, I would buy a CD or cassette and spend time carefully removing the plastic. If I didn't like the music I would re-wrap it, sometimes with the help of glue or scotch tape, and try to get a refund or an exchange. This behavior re-created the same feeling when I got when I shoplifted because I knew I was being dishonest and was trying to "beat the system." Nowadays, I buy fewer cassettes or CD's and that's okay. I gave up my need to have the latest music, the latest everything.

If something I buy breaks due to my own fault, I try to allow myself to feel my anger, frustration, and disappointment. Sometimes I fall into the trap of "beating myself up" about it. That's my controlling, perfectionist part. But generally, I feel, yell, talk and, if need be, go back to the store after I've cooled off and explain what happened openly and honestly. Usually, the store will work with me on repairing it or replacing it for free or for a discount. If they won't, I can be upset about that, too, but I need to handle it.

If I buy something and have lost the receipt, I usually try to take it back without the receipt and see if they will work with me. Very often they will. If I buy something and decide at some point, I don't like it or want it and I know I can't return or exchange it, I either give it as a gift or to charity and chalk it up as a lesson to not buy impulsively. I realize I am human and allow myself to take some risks buying things (music, books, food, etc.) that I may not like later. This is part of letting go of control.

Most addicts, particularly shoplifters, have an intense need for control and for things--even in small instances--not to go wrong. Sometimes, the smaller the instance the more aggravating the feeling.

Changing/Switching Price Tags

This is stealing. I've done it a few times, some shoplifting addicts engage in this routinely, some exclusively. The addict mind rationalizes that changing or switching price tags to lower the cost of merchandise is less of an evil than shoplifting the merchandise outright. *Tell that one to the judge!* The law still views it as retail fraud or shoplifting. It can be just as addicting and rush-producing. Most likely, switching price tags in time will lead to shoplifting merchandise outright.

Sampling Food/Taking Food

Each store's policy varies. You need to know that it is possible to be arrested and charged with shoplifting for sampling food not specifically labeled or displayed "for sampling." We had a mother and a daughter sent to C.A.S.A. who were arrested and convicted for sampling grapes at a Meijer's supermarket. No kidding. It may be "everybody does it" but the safest way is to ask an employee if you may sample some of the food product.

I'm a "sampleaholic." When I'm in a store which offers samples, I enjoy taking them up on that. But I must not abuse it. It is a relatively safe and legal way to enjoy freebies. Recently, I was at my favorite market where my wife and I spend a lot of money. They routinely offer samples of food (bread, dips, fruit, chips, cheese, etc.) I was enjoying this privilege and, admittedly, went overboard by making a second round around the market, trying a few things a second time. An employee must have noticed me--I wasn't trying to be sneaky--and asked "Are you going to sample your way through the whole store, sir?" I was taken aback and my anger rose in part to cover my embarrassment. Without hesitation I turned to her and responded "Why yes, yes I am!" It felt empowering to say that as I felt she was rude to talk to me, a customer, that way. However, part of me saw her point. I almost reported her rudeness to the manger but let it go. In my active addiction, that was just the kind of excuse--a rude employee--I needed to justify shoplifting from the store.

Taking sugars, other condiments from restaurants or markets is a behavior to be on guard for. It is best to practice asking if you can have a few to take with you. Do it.

Sneaking into the Movies

When I first stopped shoplifting I occasionally sneaked into movie theaters without paying or stayed for a second show after having paid for one. This can get you arrested for trespassing, or at least, humiliated and banned from the theater. If you think it might be wrong, it probably is.

Today, I see a lot fewer movies. They are expensive, I'm more active and busy, and I choose other forms of entertainment and escape. I go to matinees or after-run cinemas (the dollar shows), wait for some movies to come on cable TV, pay-per-view, or rent videos or DVD's at stores or libraries. I no longer crave the feeling of sneaking into a theater and doubt I could really enjoy the movie if I didn't pay for it as my conscience would be nagging at me.

Me and the Parking Meters

To this day, I must have some unresolved issue with parking meters. I will pay if I have to but always feel the urge to chance not putting money in or I put a little in and then try to push getting back to the car on time. It's like a gamble. When I come back with the meter expired and no ticket, it feels like I "beat the system" and got "something for nothing." Honestly, half the time I get a ticket and then my whole evening is ruined. Then I write in letters of protest and usually get the ticket dismissed. But if I'm honest with myself, it's pretty foolish and annoying. My wife hates this about me. She always tells me: "Just pay a few dollars to park your car in the lot. It won't kill you. I don't want to ruin another night when you get a ticket." It's the little things that seem little until they become a pattern. Then they become big things.

Bending Rules and Privileges

A few years ago, I bought my first home, a condo. My wife and I joined the health club just around the corner. We decided we could only afford the racquet membership which allows us to use the hot tub, dry and wet saunas, the showers, the indoor track and, for an additional charge, play tennis. It does not include use of the nautilus equipment, the pool, the basketball courts, or the aerobics/yoga classes.

We got to know a yoga instructor who taught classes weekly at the club. She asked if we were coming to any of the classes. I was honest: "We'd love to but we only have a limited membership." She said she didn't mind if we came. I knew it wasn't totally kosher but figured the teacher said it was okay and we chose to go only to the Tuesday evening class. Three months went by and we were loving the class.

One night, I was stretching in the room before class A young, burly man I'd never seen before came up to me. He was wearing an employee shirt and asked, "Are you Terrence?" I knew something was up, braced myself, and answered. "Yes."

"I believe you're a racquet club member. You can't take these classes but if you'd like to upgrade your membership, we can do that for you today." (Translation: "If you'd like to pay a thousand dollars more a year, you can attend").

"Oh, really?" I quipped. "The instructor told us we could attend." He told me that didn't matter. "Who can I talk to?" I felt embarrassed, disappointed, and angry and wondered how they finally caught on to me. It felt like getting caught for shoplifting but not as severe. I didn't want to get kicked out of the club. I took a calculated guess if I was ever confronted for "bending the rules" I would, at least, be given a warning-- which I was. My wife went upstairs with me to see if there was some way we could be allowed just to attend this once a week class. We even offered to pay extra for the class. But rules were rules.

It took me a week to recover from this incident. I felt differently about the club, like I didn't belong there. I knew I couldn't chance bending that rule again. I played the whole thing back in my mind and imagined what I could have done differently to avoid getting caught. I felt the pain of having lost my sneaky edge. I felt the frustration of not being able to create a solution I thought was fair.

I had to let it go. My not being able to attend yoga class on Tuesday nights allowed me to take a friend's spirituality class that took place the same nights. I laughed to myself: "They say the Universe often takes away something in order to open up something new. This or something better." I rarely agree with rules but realize when I continuously break them, it sets up a shame cycle which keeps my life in turmoil, my relationships on edge and distant, and will lead to relapse in time. *Recovery means looking at all areas of my life and making changes if I want a better life.*

What rules do you bend? And what's the breaking point?

Honesty Is Its Own Reward

"Honesty is its own reward" is an old saying and I was brought up believing this. Then something went awry. First, I began to pick up on the lies going on in my family, the cover-up around my Dad's secretive drinking. I was learning, if honesty was so great, how come there were lies and secrets? I also began to experience how nice, honest guys didn't always get the girls; how nice, honest guys got taken advantage of; how nice, honest guys don't always finish first.

At some point some of us learn not to be so naive and rigid about every rule of life. But I cracked and went the other way, I gave up on honesty to a large degree. This allowed me to shoplift and steal. But I'd always feel some guilt afterwards so I knew stealing was wrong. And I continued to be honest in most other ways. I told the truth about other things and I rarely stole from individuals, mainly stores and some workplaces.

Today I have come full circle and realize that honesty brings with it trust and peace of mind. My fiancee appreciates my honesty, my Mom and stepfather trust me, my workplace trusted me enough to hire me and keep me knowing I was a recovering shoplifter. It feels freeing to be honest, to not have to look over your shoulder for fear the lies and dishonesty are catching up with you. Life is challenging enough without creating more drama.

I have a story. Once, while Director of a chemical dependency clinic, a young client brought me a check in an envelope that our company had written to a local business. He claimed he found it on the ground and expected to be acknowledged for his honesty--financially. He was truly amazed when I just gave him a heartfelt thank you and a smile. He couldn't believe it. He felt this was a breakthrough for him--actually returning a check instead of trying to cash it as he apparently had done before. He said this much to me. I admit, he was so persuasive I was tempted to give him a reward out of guilt. But, instead, I told him to sit with just the acknowledgment of his honest behavior. He went away. The following day he came back to the office for his counseling treatment and told me he had gotten the lesson.

By this time, the staff had discussed this event and decided to give him a gift of some sort to show our appreciation for his growth. He was pleasantly surprised when, after letting go of his feelings that we had been unfair, he got a reward on top of his own reward for being honest.

Honesty promotes:

*Trust
*Self-esteem
*Being given responsibilities
*Good relationships
*Serenity
*Others being honest with you
*Spiritual connectedness
*Admiration and respect

Losing Your Edge or Gaining Your Edge?

During my therapy and periodically since, it would sometimes pain me to think of stopping shoplifting as "losing my edge." After all, I still had beliefs that good guys are boring and don't win in life. To throw in the towel was to give-up my "edge," my capacity to tread the line of fearlessness.

I've come to realize that the real edge is learning how to be myself. The real edge is having nowhere to run to when feeling angry, depressed or anxious. The real edge is surrendering control over the need for control, over the manipulating of life from moment to moment. The ultimate edge is learning how to be where I need to be. I still find that hard at times. I still fall into the familiar trap of expecting things to go my way if I am good, if I do the right thing, if I am honest. Sometimes they do, but not always. There's no guarantees.

I have an edge in recovery that is much more real than when I was a shoplifting addict. My edge is more in full view that behind the scenes or exhibited through the occasional biting joke or remark. My edge is in my ability to be present.

I've had to grieve some loss of "slickness" I honed during my days of shoplifting and stealing. I'm sure if I went into a store today to shoplift I would be much more nervous, clumsy, and more likely to get caught. I don't dwell on this, though. I also find that I can still be slick in my attorney-like way with arguments and getting out of other jams like parking tickets. Recovery reminds me I have chosen a different path.

Be Assertive!

I am convinced most people shoplift as an indirect substitute for not asking for what they really want. Most of us have been trained not to be selfish, to put our needs last. We are not taught how to speak up for what we want and need. We are not taught to be assertive. We either remain passive, become violent or aggressive at times, or–more frequently–act out passive-aggressively through shoplifting and stealing. We take out our anger or other feelings on the store: that's indirect, it doesn't deal with the source. I'd say one of the top three topics at C.A.S.A. meetings is how to be more assertive in our relationships–with spouses, family, children, friends, the boss, co-workers, everybody. There are many good books on how to be more assertive. I recommend finding one that works for you.

My wife and I dined at a restaurant about a year ago. I had a two-for-one coupon. We arrived at 6:15, had a leisurely talk before ordering our food a little after 6:30. When I gave the waitress the coupon at the end of the meal, she came back and told me I wouldn't be able to use it because there was a restriction on it: it was a Friday night, there was some fine print which stated it could only be used for "seating before 6:30pm." I hadn't even noticed the fine print but told her we had been sat at 6:15 anyway. She said that seating meant the time when you ordered your food and, apparently, we hadn't ordered until about 6:40. I felt my blood start to boil. I composed myself and asked to speak to the manager. She left, returned a few minutes later, and told me that I could use the coupon after all. I felt good about asserting myself.

Have you asserted yourself lately?

The Importance of Humor

Having a sense of humor about my life and life in general has been and continues to be one of my biggest challenges. Most addicts have a great sense of humor yet are incredibly sensitive and often take too much in, let too much affect them. They take on the world's pain at an early age, going from caring too much to caring too little. This has to change; in time, a healthy balance will arise.

Given the pain and injustice many of us feel, the hardest thing is to laugh at ourselves. How do we do that? First: We need to look at whether clinical depression or a chemical imbalance contributes to our doldrums and get that checked out. Secondly: What probably keeps us from laughing is all the energy we block when holding onto the past and/or fearing the future. *It's hard to laugh when we deny our present feelings and experiences. Laughter and joy live in the present moment.* If you've ever caught yourself in a good belly laugh, you'll recall that you let go of your attachment to the past and to future. You were in the moment. True comedy is an art and a gift. It gives us back the gift of the present.

So what's so funny about being a shoplifting addict? Not much if you are in the throes of it. But can you at least see the absurdity of believing that your peace and salvation comes from stealing objects from stores or others? It is sad to admit but true. You are not alone. Haven't you ever thought of someone else's behaviors as ridiculous or childish? It's time to turn the mirror on yourself, as hard as that might be. *The truth will set you free. But first it might piss you off.*

Many addicts have learned to use humor as a defense mechanism or cover-up to protect themselves from pain. The class clown is a good example. These attention seekers often succeed in life until their pain can no longer remain concealed. "Fake it till you make it" is a popular saying. This can work for a while; after all, people fake through their pain by shoplifting and stealing. We need to hang around upbeat, positive people who help uplift us while we feel into the darkest depths of our pain. We need to pace ourselves. We can't rush the healing, we can't rush the laughter. But we can do the two-step: Do some hard work, give ourselves a break and have some fun.

I remain a recovering "serious person." For those of us who grew up early and took on being reliable, responsible and self-sacrificing, the anger and pain takes a while to melt and give way to lightness, spontaneity and joy. Others before us have been able to realize this. What do you think prevents us from experiencing this? Most likely, our own ego and stubbornness. This is recovery: letting go of the belief that life is unfair, cruel, unsafe, and empty.

"Let go and let God" is a favorite saying in recovery circles. But what does it mean? And how do you do it? I refer back to Step 1 and admit "I am powerless." I'm out there in the world trying to accomplish things, trying to make things happen. When things aren't working out the way I'd like them to, I have choices: I can get angry or upset, I can keep trying, I can do both, or I can give up and quit.

In recovery from shoplifting, I remember how difficult it was for me in therapy to "Let go and let God." I wasn't able to trust there even was a God, a benevolent force or any kind of plan where the details of life could be handled if I just let go. If I stopped shoplifting, how would I survive financially? If I stopped shoplifting, how would I survive emotionally? Shoplifting was my crutch. Recovery had become my support. Letting go is an ongoing process.

Today I can laugh at myself about my shoplifting. It doesn't mean I don't feel the pain of it but I am grateful for what my addiction experience has taught me. I am glad I took my lemons from life and made lemonade. Sometimes people will make jokes about my history of shoplifting and stealing. Depending on who it is and the context of the joke, I am usually able to laugh right along with them. I recognized the joke inherent with publishing a book on shoplifting: If it's ever in the stores, how am I going to make any money off it–everybody's going to shoplift it. Sometimes I will introduce myself to people and tell them I'm in recovery from shoplifting addiction, I'll reach into my back pocket and produce my wallet and ask them with a smile: "Is this your wallet?" They almost always begin to check their back pocket or purse.

I love to tell jokes and most people know me as a jokester. The people closest to me, however, see the other side: the overly serious side. Nonetheless, one of my little known passions is to be a stand-up comedian. I do write funny songs on the guitar and perform them at parties. I get a lot of affirmation for that.

How do you find humor? What makes you laugh?

Forgiving Ourselves

It's hard forgiving others who we have harmed us. It's hard forgiving life, God, the world, for not living up to our hopes and expectations. Forgiving ourselves, however, may be the hardest journey of all.

I'm tremendously self-critical. The tape is always there, playing in my head. It's been hard to forgive myself for things I did in the past. I'm no longer holding onto any guilt or shame over hurting the stores any of the people in my life. It's more about forgiving myself for being human, making mistakes.

"Shame" stands for:

SHOULD
HAVE
ALREADY
MASTERED
EVERYTHING

I forgive myself for being jealous of my brother.
I forgive myself for not being a better son to my Dad.
I forgive myself for not being the perfect, religious little boy my grandmother wanted.
I forgive myself for crying when my friends teased me.
I forgive myself for being shy around girls.
I forgive myself for stealing and shoplifting.

I forgive myself. I forgive myself. I forgive myself.

What do you need to forgive yourself for?

Part Three

Exercises

Questions for Self-Exploration

1. Recall your earliest memory of stealing something that didn't belong to you. What did you take?

2. What was going on in your life at the time that may have been significant?

3. What did you think and feel about your action?

4. Was there anything symbolic about what you stole?

5. Were there any negative or positive consequences from your action?

6. Did you develop a habit of stealing things soon afterwards or later? If so, how long?

7. When you were a child, did you witness someone else steal or engage in dishonesty? What was the stolen?

8. What was going on in your life at the time that may have been significant?

9. What did you think and feel about this other person's action(s)?

10. Are you aware of any negative or positive consequences for that person or for you because of that person's action(s)?

11. Did you develop a habit of stealing things soon afterwards or later? If so, how long?

12. When you were a child, do you recall any incidents of things having been stolen from you literally or symbolically? What was stolen?

13. Did you know who stole this from you? If so, who?

14. What was going on in your life at this time that was significant?

15. What did you think and feel about having something stolen from you?

16. What did you think and feel about yourself?

17. What did you think and feel about the person(s) who stole from you?

18. Are there particular kinds of things that you steal? What are they and why do you steal these kind of things?

19. Are there particular places you go to steal? Where and why?

20. Have you noticed that you began to steal more things, larger things, more expensive things, or more frequently over time?

21. Are you more prone to stealing things at a particular time of the day, week, year? If so, when and why?

22. Are you more prone to stealing things when you are in a certain mood? Anxious? Angry? Lonely? Depressed? Manic?

23. Are you more prone to stealing things when a certain event or circumstance occurs? If so, explain.

24. Do you actually use or derive benefit from the objects stolen? Explain.

25. Are you able to distinguish between your desire for an object and your need for it? If so, explain.

26. Do you experience strong feelings or physical sensations right before, during, or right after you've stolen something? If so, describe the sensations and when they occur.

27. Do you tend to be perfectionist and in need of control or order? If so, do you think this is a factor in why you steal?

28. Do you recognize any other addictive or compulsive behaviors in your life? What are they and how do they relate to your stealing?

29. Who knows about your stealing and to what extent?

30. What prevents you from telling certain persons or from elaborating to the ones you have told?

31. List all the benefits, financial and emotional, that you have gotten out of stealing? Be honest with yourself.

32. List all the costs, financial and emotional, that you have gotten out of stealing. Be honest with yourself.

33. Do you want to stop stealing? Why and why not?

34. What are you prepared to do to support yourself in stopping and not starting again?

35.What have you learned about yourself from these questions?

My List of Unfair Things

Acknowledge that you feel like a victim and feel it as fully as you need to. But also acknowledge that you cannot change the past and you cannot control the future. Acknowledge that, in some way, this is what you have been attempting to do with shoplifting--undo or make-up for the past and buffer future pain and disappointment. And you got hooked. I got hooked. We got hooked. Where do we go from here?

What if we surrendered the notion of fairness altogether? What if we learn to live life on life's terms and accept that sometimes things go well, sometimes better than we thought, and sometimes they don't go as we wish? For "recovering victims" like me I know what it feels like to feel like life rarely or never goes my way, like I'm not getting my reward, like I am being cursed or punished. It is a very painful way to live but, at least, I get to be right about it and have plenty of evidence to support this.

There are still too many days when I'd rather be right than be happy. So much of the world falls into this trap. When do we really get to enjoy life? Can we ever just attune to a place of wonder, surrender, letting go and living in the moment? And if so, why doesn't it seem to last? I need to be careful about dwelling on my feelings of self-pity and my thoughts about life being unfair. But making a list of these helps put in out there in a concrete way for me (and others if I want) to take a look at it. *The goal is not to dwell in the list but to name it feel it, and release it.* Some may wish to burn or bury the list afterward.

My List of Unfair Things

1. My Dad was alcoholic
2. My parents got divorced
3. I grew up with a lisp

4. My cousins had more money than we did, a normal family
5. I had to take care of my Mom & brother and had to grow up
6. I wasn't allowed in my friend's tree house because my Dad was a lawyer
7. My bike, skateboard, & comic books were stolen from me
8. My Dad and Mom never got back together
9. My little brother disobeyed me
10. We had to give our dog away because she bit a neighbor
11. My Dad got remarried and had a son without asking me how I felt about it
12. My face broke out badly in high school
13. Sally broke up with me though I was a perfect gentleman
14. My Dad made me take out student loans for college
15. My friend got all the girls and he was a jerk
16. My friend got the job that I was better qualified for
17. My Dad had a severe stroke just as we were getting close
18. There were no support groups for recovering shoplifters
19. My Dad died at age 53
20. My book proposal got rejected (many times)

Think of all those things you hate about your life or feel are unfair. Really run with it! Don't hold back or edit yourself out of guilt. We've all been told not to complain or whine. Let it rip! Your intention is to get it out so you can let it go. What's the worst that can happen? You'll either end up in tears of sadness or tears of laughter, or both!

Your List of Unfair Things (Go for it!)

1.

2.

3.

4.

5.

6.

7.

8.

9.

10.

11.

12.

13.

14.

15.

16.

17.

18.

19.

20.

My Lucky Gratitude List

No matter how bad you feel your life has been, there is another side of the coin. You are still alive. You may not view that as a good thing. But recovery requires us to begin thinking in a new way. When someone comes to C.A.S.A. devastated from a recent shoplifting arrest, sure their life is over, that the judge is going to lock them up forever, their family is going to disown them, they're going to lose their job, their home, their future--it reminds me of the power of thought. In my 11 years of hearing these stories, the worst has never happened. That's not to say people didn't lose things–they did–but most of the time things turned out much better. Many come to be grateful for their shoplifting addiction and arrest(s): it steered them toward help and toward a greater appreciation of basic gifts: freedom, family, friends, health, comforts, opportunities.

We made a list of unfair things because we needed to bring that out to see what keeps us from feeling grateful, lucky. I'm a classic worrier and I lean toward pessimism easily. It's like the old joke: "What's the difference between a pessimist and an optimist? An optimist thinks this is the best of all possible worlds. A pessimist knows that it is." Or another way of saying it: "An optimist's creed is, gratefully, 'It doesn't get any better than this.' A pessimist's creed is, ungratefully, 'It doesn't get any better than this.'"

Is the glass half-full or half-empty is a trick question. Why even look at the glass like that? If there's water in it, be thankful there's water in it. If it's empty, why not be grateful there's a glass there to catch the water from wherever it comes?

My Lucky Gratitude List

1. I am still alive (hopefully, you consider this good fortune given all those who have died)

2. My mother is happy and healthy
3. I won an art award in high school
4. I was named salutatorian in high school
5. I won the MVP trophy for flag football during the Summer before I went to high school
6. I didn't die in a car accident in 1991
7. I have a step-father who loves me and is a good role model
8. I had a support group to help me start C.A.S.A.
9. I met my mentor and therapist through starting C.A.S.A.
10. My therapist introduced me to men's groups where I met some of my best friends
11. I have healed wounds with my younger brother
12. My mom and step dad have supported my leaving my job
13. I have a wonderful wife who treats me well
14. I left my job on good terms
15. I have a wonderful community of friends
16. I have enough money to publish this book
17. I won door prizes three times at my business meeting
18. I haven't been arrested in over 13 years!
19. I have an opportunity to help others
20. I got to write a song on my guitar when the power went off

Think about any lucky breaks you've had in life. Think of things that could have been worse but they're not. It's time to put your thinking cap on. If you are having trouble, ask someone close to you to prod you in the right direction.

Your Lucky Break/Gratitude List: (Just Do It!)

1.

2.

3.

4.

5.

6.

7.

8.

9.

10.

11.

12.

13.

14.

15.

16.

17.

18.

19.

20.

A List of Ways to Avoid the Stores

1. Have others shop for you
2. Shop by mail
3. Shop by Internet
4. Call stores and have them prepare goods, food for pick-up
5. Create, recycle gifts at home for yourself or others
6. Go to garage sales or flea markets where you are less inclined to steal from "individuals" vs. stores
7. Develop new hobbies to occupy your time (walking, movies, exercise, art, writing, new business projects)
8. Go through your home and rediscover what you can still use or appreciate: clothes, music, books, food, toiletries
9. Learn to barter with others for services
10. Gratitude prayers: "I already have what I need" "I am worth more than stealing can provide" "I am provided for"
11. Stay home in your pajamas
12. Call a friend for support
13. Get rid of clothing, purses or other items which helped you conceal items to shoplift
14. Commit to avoid stores from which you have shoplifted-- you don't need to return to the scene of the crime--move on
15. Immerse yourself in a project, hobby, or neglected goal
16. Be with people you won't go to stores or shoplift with
17. Have yourself banned from certain stores by going there with a loved one and telling them you have a problem. (Problem gamblers can ban themselves from casinos)

Add some of your ideas to this list:

18.

19.

20.

If you have to go to a store, here are some next level defenses you can use to minimize your temptation to shoplift:

1. Carry a stone in your pocket or hand for comfort, strength.
2. Carry a picture of a child or loved one to look at to remind you of who loves you.
3. Carry a book of worship or inspiration to help center you.
4. Leave your purse, bring a small purse, or don't empty your purse out
5. Wear tight-fitting clothes which could not conceal items well
6. Do not walk in with empty or half-empty bags or backpacks
7. Keep your hands in your pockets
8. Make a shopping list before you go in, keep it out, keep to it
9. Create a budget first and then have enough cash in hand
10. Pay by check, money order, debit or credit card if that helps.

Add some of your ideas:

11.

12.

13.

14.

15.

16.

17.

18.

19.

20.

Journaling

Journaling is an important tool for many people but, especially, for recovering persons. Journaling may include diary-like writing, poems, doodles or drawings, recording of dreams, checklists. Journaling allows you to look back more objectively and clearly, notice important patterns over time. It's a great way to voice or vent whatever you're going through.

Journal Example #1

Today I am getting up and doing my best to not shoplift. I pray I can do it. I feel afraid. I feel depressed. I feel lonely. I feel empty. I know shoplifting would pick me up a little bit. It is very tempting to hop in my car, drive to the store and just zone in and zone out. But I am trying to change my life. I have to have faith there is another way. It's so hard for me to trust that right now. There are people around me who seem to be able to do it but I always think: "I'm different. I can't do it. I don't want to do it. I'm scared to do it. There's something different about me." I don't trust that life can get better. Sometimes I do, but most of the time I don't. And I feel very ashamed about this. I just want everything to be okay. It seems like it never is. I know I can't control life but I wish I could. I don't know the secret to being happy. Sometimes happiness seems so far away. All I know is I don't want to die. Even when I feel like dying, I really want to live. There's a part of me inside that really just wants to love and be loved. Maybe it's the child in me who never got to fully experience the innocence and wonder of life. Now I'm an adult and it seems like there's too much responsibility: bills to be paid, relationships, work. Everything seems like a chore I don't know how to play this game. It seems like I always get one step ahead and then: Bam! I'm back to square one again. Stealing doesn't even work for me anymore. It just complicates my life and makes me more anxious and depressed. It creates more pain for me and for others. I don't know how to be happy yet but I know how to stop creating new pain in my life. I have enough to work on now. I wish I had more money. I wish I had more power. I wish I was more excited, more connected. It seems so hard. I guess I need to just take baby steps today. Recovery is a trip. I need to forgive myself for giving up. I want to try again.

Journal Example #2

Today was rough. I didn't think I'd make it through. I can count at least five times I was tempted to take something. I wish this bug would go away. It's gotta get easier. The first time was this morning at the gas station. I knew I should have gotten gas last night when I had more time. I was rushed and the damned pump wasn't turning on and then it finally did but when I went in to pay there was this long line and my first thought was "Shit, I can't believe this! Why don't they have more help? I'm gonna be late for work!" I know looking back on it now that I am partly to blame. I was running late myself. I know it's not an ideal world we live in. Everyone's in a hurry all the time. I had to slow down. I could have enjoyed that time and even read a magazine or struck up a conversation with someone in line. But, instead, I just thought of walking out and not paying for the gas. Fortunately, I talked myself out of that. Then I was up at the counter paying for the gas and I had to keep from looking at the gum and candy on the counter. I noticed a quarter in the little container where they keep the pennies for those who need them or those who wish to leave them. I wanted to take it but didn't. By the time I got back to my car I couldn't wait to hit the road. On the radio, all I heard was the morning's depressing news. Shut it off, rolled down the window and enjoyed the sound, smell and feel of the wind blowing by me. I was in a peaceful place. Somehow I made it to work on time and took a deep breath before going in the building. I said a little prayer. I prayed for protection from any bad energy that might come my way that day, that it not affect me, that I not absorb it.

Things were going well at work until the end of the day when I was coming up the stairs and I overheard a conversation by two female co-workers who were complaining about me, belittling me. It was like a spear harpooned through my heart. I stopped in my tracks and wondered what to do. Part of me wanted to slink back down the stairs without them knowing. Part of me wanted to run up and tell them to "Fuck off!" But the hurt and wounded part of me wanted them to know how much I was hurt. So I walked up the stairs slowly until I stood in front of them. They could tell I heard them. They were silent. I told them softly but sternly "I heard that." I went into my office and didn't know what to do.

In the old days, I'm not sure what I would have done but I probably would have gone to a store and shoplifted myself silly, just like the alcoholic goes to the bar. Instead, went back downstairs, got in my car, and drove around. I pulled over after a few minutes and started banging on the steering wheel, yelling every swear word in the book. Then I started to cry. After a good five minutes, my whole body seemed to drop. I took the rest of the day off, went to the gym to work out, took a hot tub and sauna. I called my buddy Lee up on the phone and vented. I'm glad he's my friend.

I feel angry when you don't appreciate me.
I feel hurt when you bring up the past
I feel sad when you don't pay attention to me
I feel afraid when we have trouble paying the bills on time
I feel happy when we have quality time and don't criticize

Practice Journal Page

Make a List of Your Gray Area Behaviors

List all your gray area dishonest behaviors. Be honest with yourself if with nobody else. Write down your rationalizations for engaging in these behaviors. Write down your perceived benefits from engaging in these behaviors. Then write down the negative costs or potential consequences of each.

Sample List

1. Switching price tags
2. Returning merchandise by trick
3. Sampling food
4. Petty office theft
5. Beating the parking meters
6. Not correcting cashier mistakes
7. Not returning lost and found items
8. Incorrectly reporting taxes
9. Sneaking into movies
10. Creating perks at clubs that are not allowed

List your gray area behaviors:

1.

2.

3.

4.

5.

6.

7.

8.

9.

10.

EXAMPLE

<u>Gray Area Behavior</u>

I. Stealing office supplies from the office for personal use

<u>*Rationalizations*</u>

1. It's not stealing
2. Everybody does it
3. The company can afford it
4. I am using these at work
5. I do other things for free for my company
6. It's a small perk
7. Property should be shared
8. As long as it's only a little, it's okay
9. I deserve a little reward or something extra
10. I don't have time to go to the post office

<u>*Perceived Benefits*</u>

1. I get a good feeling of getting a little something extra
2. It saves me time on going to the store, my time is valuable
3. It keeps me from taking bigger things at the office
4. It keeps me from shoplifting
5. I avoid conflict because I am getting something back
6. It helps me put up with the low pay–I reward myself
7. It comforts me to know I have this support system to help me
8. It's the one thing I look forward to coming to work for

<u>*Costs/Consequences*</u>

1. Keeps me looking over my shoulder, afraid of getting caught
2. Could be embarrassing if I am discovered
3. Could be fired if I am found out

4. Feel ashamed, secretive, loss of good eye contact
5. Compromises my recovery
6. Feel hypocritical
7. Deprives me of the chance to directly feel feelings, deal with issues, live life on life's terms
8. Deprives me of practice being assertive at work as it becomes easier to keep quiet, unnoticed

Notes:

Healthier Ways to Get Freebies & Good Deals

We all love a bargain. We all love to get something for nothing. Be creative and come up with some safe, fun, natural alternatives to fill that need *occasionally:*

Examples:

1. Coupons
2. Flea Markets/Thrift Stores
3. Only buy sale items
4. Go to free sample days
5. Create art or functional items through creativity
6. Festivals, art/health fairs often offer free stuff
7. Garage sales
8. Estate sales
9. Volunteer for experiment studies
10. Auctions

Caution:

I encourage the use of these alternatives as legal, enjoyable substitutes for "something for nothing." But each person's recovery is different. For some, these alternatives may not be appropriate. People with addictive personalities, by nature, tend not to be able to easily moderate and balance.

I've met a few people who have "coupon addiction." They obsess about gathering coupons, saving coupons, using coupons, altering coupons, hoarding coupons. This is real and can interfere with your life. You can end up spending more money with coupons as you may not have needed to buy anything but did because you couldn't resist the lure of the savings. You felt guilty, upset, ashamed afterward. It's not worth it and may trigger shoplifting urges. This is how coupons work--they lure you in. Coupons can give you a false sense of abundance

I use coupons from the dining entertainment book I buy each year for about $40. Even when using a two-for one coupon at a moderately priced restaurant, I always think I'm going to end up paying just $10 or so but end up paying at least $20 once I pay tip on both meals, drinks, and appetizer and/or dessert.

Our friend Sandra used to buy and sell at flea markets. Her basement became filled with boxes of knickknacks and created stress in her marriage. Her flea marketing ended up costing a lot of time, money and energy which could have been spent elsewhere in a more productive, life-enhancing manner.

---

*I credit Terence Gorski for following work on Triggers, Warning Signs and the exercise "How My Addiction Served Me." I also thank Personalized Nursing LIGHT House, Inc., for having employed me as a counselor to teach this material to many clients over several years.

Common Triggers and Ways to Cope

Triggers are stimuli I encounter in my external environment, namely, people, places, things, or events--that can set off a chain reaction of thoughts and feelings leading to a shoplifting or stealing relapse. Recovery requires avoiding these triggers which put me at risk, developing coping skills to deal with them if/when they enter my space. This will require lifestyle changes.

Some examples of my triggers and coping skills include:

I. People

1. *My Dad (because when I saw him, I'd often feel angry, guilty, sad, depressed, anxious) especially when he drank*

Coping skills:

1. avoid or limit contact or length of visits
2. have a heart to heart with him about how I feel
3. journal about my feelings
4. talk about issues in C.A.S.A. or A.C.O.A. groups
5. work on issues in therapy or in men's groups
6. talk to family/friends about my feelings
7. use self-talk/affirmations while visiting
8. do deep breathing as feelings come up & leave
9. do something calming before and/or after visiting him(work out, take a hot tub/sauna, go for a walk, etc.)
10. be assertive about boundaries and what behaviors I won't tolerate

---

2. Certain friends or family (I had to avoid or limit time with certain friends who still were engaged in other addictions to alcohol, pot, or even TV because they sucked me into the negative and addictive energy patterns which depressed me)

143

Coping skills:

1. avoid or limit contact with such friends
2. have a heart to heart with them that right now you will need some space to work on your issues/recovery
3. make new friends in other social groups, hobby groups, or recovery groups
4. find other ways to make connections (e-mail, letter, phone)
5. do volunteer work to be around others
6. make friends with coworkers
7. develop solitary hobbies
8. get a pet or spend more time with the one you have
9. commune with nature more
10. journal

II. Places

1. Stores (obviously)

Coping skills:

1. avoid or limit trips to stores
2. develop new places to spend time (gym, movies, museums, your own home)
3. ask others to help you with shopping (go with them if you are less likely to steal when with others but it is best to avoid stores altogether)
4. shop by mail, by Internet, or call ahead to pickup groceries, carry-out food
5. subscribe to magazines by mail
6. shop at new places where you are unlikely to steal (flea markets or charities)
7. keep smooth rock in your pocket as a reminder

8. create your own art, clothing, grow food in a garden, make useable items
9. join a health club to keep me out of stores (I won't have as much money left over for shopping anyway)
10. tell the storekeepers I am a recovering shoplifter so they can keep an eye on me to deter me.

III. Things

1. *Overcoat, cassette tapes, certain magazines, comic books, skateboards, newspapers sitting outside stores or on peoples' front porches (things that I had shoplifted or stolen or things that had been stolen from me earlier in life)*

Coping skills:

1. avoid contact with if possible
2. if encountered and feeling agitated, do breathing and self-talk and leave
3. aversion therapy with therapist or self if strong
4. find new objects to enjoy that have no painful history
5. remind self that possessing the object will not bring happiness
6. journal about my feelings/experience
7. talk about it at my support group
8. find other things to do to take my mind off it
9. give myself a new, better kind of treat or reward
10. yell or exercise to burn off any tension created

IV. Events

1. *Information or changes like I get fired or laid-off from my job, someone close to me dies or becomes ill, a romantic partner breaks up with me, I get a promotion or I move my home--even "positive" change can create stress and feelings of loss of control and fear. Anniversary dates or holidays are also events. An example of a triggering event was my father's stroke just two months after I started law school and had stopped stealing and turned over a new leaf.*

Coping skills:

1. increase my awareness immediately that this is a major event that could bring up strong emotions and potential relapse
2. make an appointment with a therapist
3. stay out of stores
4. make sure I am not alone for long
5. journal my feelings
6. pray and meditate
7. attend a support group
8. don't isolate, hang out with good friends
9. work out at health club, take sauna, hot tub
10. see psychiatrist for medication if need be

Common Warning Signs and Ways to Cope

Warning signs are stimuli in my internal environment (thoughts, feelings) as well as behavior patterns (lying, for example) which are like red flags. If unchecked, they build-up and will contribute to a relapse of shoplifting or stealing.

I. Thoughts

1. "Life is unfair"

Coping skills:

1. notice the familiar negative thought pattern and don't give in to it
2. counter this thought with a new thought such as "Thank you for sharing" or "Yes, life feels unfair right now but stealing doesn't really help"
3. begin deep breathing
4. slow down, lay down or meditate on a new thought, your breath, or your body
5. journal the thoughts and feelings
6. talk to someone
7. engage in primal scream or go for a walk to release stress
8. pray to see things differently
9. review or make a new gratitude list
10. do volunteer work to help those less fortunate

II. Feelings

1. Anger

Coping skills:

1. notice the familiar feeling pattern, don't judge it, but don't give into it
2. begin deep breathing

3. allow yourself to feel the feeling fully
4. allow yourself to release the feeling cleanly and harmlessly
5. engage in primal scream or anger release like breaking a stick or hitting a pillow
6. talk to a therapist or friend
7. exercise
8. cry
9. journal
10. talk to somebody

III. Behaviors

1. Isolating, beginning to engage in "gray area" dishonesty, becoming passive and stuffing anger instead of asserting myself, judging others, stopping going to meetings, care taking

Coping skills:

1. notice the familiar behavioral pattern, acknowledge its danger
2. begin deep breathing
3. ask yourself why you are doing this; are you really committed to your recovery?
4. speak with a therapist, friend, or sponsor
5. journal about it
6. go to a movie (but don't sneak in)
7. create something artistic
8. go for a long walk
9. start moving your body and let sound come out
10. clean, organize, do a project

Make a list of your top ten triggers & coping skills:

Triggers   Coping Skills

1.

2.

3.

4.

5.

6.

7.

8.

9.

10.

Make a list of your top ten warning signs & coping skills:

Warning Signs   Coping Skills

1.

2.

3.

4.

5.

6.

7.

8.

9.

10.

How My Addiction Served Me

Be honest. You know you were getting something out of your addiction. Despite the negative consequences, despite the attempts to stop and the powerlessness to do so, all addictions serve the addict. There is a payoff, a perceived benefit. It is crucial to get clear on this not only to increase your self-knowledge but to better implement ways to meet the needs you were trying to fill by shoplifting.

A key to recovery is developing new ways to cope with issues, new ways to get needs met. This takes patience and discipline because the addict has gotten used to trying to get quick fixes to needs and has developed a robotic or automatic way of doing this.

For Example:

I. *Shoplifting helped comfort me when I was angry*

*Payoff: It protected me from my anger because I was afraid to feel it or release it on others

*Cost: By using shoplifting as a way to suppress/avoid my anger, I now realize it continued to build like a pressure cooker. I was still angry and always on edge. I'm sure my blood pressure went up and I had other symptoms from holding in my anger. I deprived myself of learning of how to set boundaries, how to say "no," how to express my anger in healthier ways. Thus, my people pleasing continued because I knew I could just go out and express my anger by shoplifting. I was arrested, though. It cost me money for court and lawyers and therapists. I kept myself emotionally stuck and immature. I alienated people because they could feel my anger underneath and which often leaked out in the form of sarcasm, cynicism, put-downs.

*New way to serve need. I still get angry. I still have a need to manage my anger. I have chosen to work on my anger and my rage from past unresolved issues as well as when anger comes up in the present. I worked on this in therapy, in support groups and men's groups, I journaled, I did anger release and primal scream work. I remind myself that anger is not bad, it is there as a messenger to tell me something needs addressing or expressing. Today when I get angry and need comfort I will first, notice I am angry and recognize this is a potentially dangerous feeling. I will stay out of stores. I will talk to my fiancée or a friend. I will share my anger at support groups. I will breathe, go for a walk, go to the health club, visit the chiropractor, get a massage. Sometimes, I admit, I will just pout, stay stuck, turn on the TV and sometimes overeat. Still, while not the healthiest coping skills, I have learned, at least, that shoplifting and stealing don't help. They only make things worse. I remind myself of that and tell myself, "this, too, shall pass." There is usually fear and sadness behind my anger.

II. *I shoplifted to fill the void of loss*

*Payoff: It helped distract me from the pain of the loss. It made me feel full for a while, complete. It numbed the pain. It filled the hole. It numbed the sadness, the anger

*Cost: By shoplifting to fill the void of many losses in my life (parents'divorce, loss of childhood, loss of romance, loss of hope), I realize I didn't allow myself to go through the necessary grieving process we all have to go through. I felt I was taking care of myself by not dealing with the grief but I wasn't. I stayed stuck. My heart began to close up. It became hard for me to let new relationships and new opportunities into my life. Instead of filling a void, I had created a bigger void. Whatever I had lost in my life, by not feeling the feelings and working through them, my fear increased.

151

*New way to serve need: There is an old saying: "All of life is about having and losing." I now see that grieving is a normal, even if painful, part of life. When my Dad died in 1993, I attended a grief support group for two years. I did a lot of reading about grief and the grieving process so I could understand what I needed to experience. Nobody teaches us about grief. I needed a roadmap. I needed validation for my feelings, especially my anger over my losses. If I am tempted to shoplift to fill the void of grief, I need to fill the void with something healthier. Besides support groups, there is counseling, creating meaningful rituals (going to grave side, lighting a candle, talking about the good times).

III. *I shoplifted to feel power, to feel control*

*Payoff: Most of us like to feel we have some control over life's circumstances. Very often, unfortunately, we don't. It can be scary and frustrating until we surrender and learn how to cope with things as best as we can. I used shoplifting to create the illusion that I was in control. It was powerful, too. First and foremost, if I was feeling a feeling I didn't like (boredom, depression, anxiety, anger, sadness, loneliness) I couldn't control those feelings. They just came up. But I learned I could control them if I shoplifted. I could shut them off. I was not able to control my Dad's drinking, my parents' getting a divorce, girls liking me, people appreciating me. But I could get something back--at least it seemed--by shoplifting. And it made me feel special and powerful: to not have to wait in line to pay for something; to not have to wait, period, if I didn't have the money on me.

*Cost: I achieved the feeling and illusion of power and control but, eventually, the tables turned and I felt more dis-empowered and out of control. It became clear to me that my very inability to stop shoplifting was a sign I had become a slave to it.

*New way to serve need: Follow-through with positive goals in my life and chart my success. Remind myself that true power comes from within, my strength of character, and from without–my Higher Power. Associate with people who help empower me and remind me of my strengths when I am down.

EXCERCISE: Complete the following payoffs, costs, and new ways to serve your needs for the following ways you identify how your shoplifting served you.

IV. *I shoplifted to lift my self-esteem when I felt inadequate*
*Payoff:

*Cost:

*New way to serve need

V. *I shoplifted to give myself a lift when I felt depressed*
*Payoff:

*Cost:

*New way to serve need:

VI. *I shoplifted to occupy myself when I was lonely*
*Payoff:

*Cost:

*New way to serve need:

VII. *I shoplifted to make life right when life seemed unfair*
*Payoff:

*Cost:

*New way to serve need:

VIII. *I shoplifted to give myself something when I felt frustrated always giving to others, it was a way to reward myself*
*Payoff:

*Cost:

*New way to serve need:

IX. *I shoplifted when I was afraid to ask for help or be assertive*

*Payoff:

*Cost:

*New way to serve need:

X. *I shoplifted because it made me feel smarter, more clever*

*Payoff:

*Cost:

*New way to serve need:

The 12 Steps & Recovery from Shoplifting Addiction

The 12 Steps have been adapted from Alcoholics Anonymous, which was founded in 1935. They can be used effectively with virtually any addiction-recovery self-help or support group. Prior to starting C.A.S.A. in 1992 I was vaguely familiar with the 12 Steps, particularly Step 1 ("We admitted we were powerless over... and our lives had become unmanageable").

However, my first support group experience was over a two year period (1991-92) when I attended S.O.S. (Secular Organization for Sobriety). This was not a 12 Step group. When I started C.A.S.A. in 1992, I adopted the more loose, more familiar model I'd learned from S.O.S. Some cross-talk is allowed, there is no Higher Power focus. Some members clearly embrace spirituality as an integral part of their recovery. C.A.S.A. touches on issues the 12 Steps outline but more loosely. We have a phone support list but no formal sponsor-sponsee system.

Over the years I have learned more about the 12 Steps. I studied them in social work school, worked with them in my own life, and taught them--to the best of my ability--as an addictions counselor since 1997. I feel different approaches to recovery exist. I look at the 12 Steps as a valuable tool. For anybody already working the Steps with any addiction, they can just as easily be applied to recovery from shoplifting addiction. For those unfamiliar with the Steps, I encourage you to study them, read literature about them, and attend a 12 Step meeting. If you decide to start a group for shoplifting addiction, the 12 Step approach has a good track record and provides some immediate structure right away.

The following are some thoughts on how one might apply the 12 Steps to recovery from addictive-compulsive shoplifting or stealing.

Step One

Admitted we were powerless over our shoplifting (stealing)-- that our lives have become unmanageable.

It took me a long time to admit this and even now, like any addict, it is easy for me to slip into the belief that I am cured and have it whipped. "Denial is not just a river in Egypt" is a popular saying in recovery circles. For a while I told myself my stealing was a choice--after all, I didn't steal everyday (not in the beginning at least) and there were periods of time where I was able to stop. This is very common. I stopped for six months after each arrest and probation. I stopped for a while each time I started a new phase of my life, like school or a relationship.

Ultimately, however, I still was powerless over stealing because I always felt the need to come back to it. Powerlessness may be measured by "not getting the lesson." Yet, by 1990, after one arrest and several confrontations by store owners, after seeing my life go downhill, and even after my second arrest, I still couldn't stop. Stealing, particularly shoplifting, had become my drug. No fear of any consequences could deter me.

I was also in denial for a long time that my life had become unmanageable. I knew things weren't always going my way--in terms of money, grades, romance, emotionally, or clarity of purpose--but I didn't realize how unmanageable things became. I was using the stealing as a way of managing my feelings, my circumstances, my conflicts, my relationships.

If getting arrested twice, feeling continuously anxious and depressed, living a secret life which could land me in jail at any moment or have me expelled from law school isn't unmanageable, then what is? For the addict, though, there always seems to be a lower bottom to hit before we wake up.

WAKE UP!

It's time to admit shoplifting has taken over your life! It has taken over. Your life has become unmanageable and stealing, when you look at it, hasn't really helped. It's hurt you and it's hurt others. It has been a life of lies, of smoke and mirrors. If stealing were the solution, why are you still depressed, anxious, unhappy, unfulfilled? What problems have multiplied? Legal? Financial? Relationship? Emotional? Work? Health? Self-esteem? Spiritual? Probably all of the above. But there is hope.

Powerless is how we felt at the start and we tried to get our power back through shoplifting or stealing. But that didn't work. We felt even more powerless over our lives and, eventually, over our shoplifting. We need to repeatedly come back to the sanity of a Step 1.

Step Two

Came to believe that a Power greater than ourselves could restore us to sanity.

Step One and Step Two came together pretty closely for me. When I hit my bottom in early 1990, having just broken up with my girlfriend and feeling on the brink of suicide, I realized how powerless I'd become over my stealing, my life, and its manageability. By some miracle, I also realized I needed help. And I asked for it. I was 25 years old and I told my parents I needed to see a counselor. For me, that was a Power greater than myself.

It is often said in recovery circles: do not make another person your Higher Power. For a short time I needed to. My therapist was my Higher Power. I had prayed to God to take away my urge to steal and that hadn't worked for me. I chose to believe God put therapists on earth to assist as well.

158

In my asking for help I must have had an inherent belief that I could also be restored to sanity; if I'd ever known sanity. I wasn't too sure about that. But I knew my life had become insane and would just get worse without help. Since then, I've been on the road to ever-increasing sanity... with a few detours along the way. I view sanity as a continuum. Many people don't know how to define sanity, much less experience it.

What does sanity mean to you? For me it means thinking and behaving in a way that really works. It means not running from nor being overwhelmed by feelings. It means living not in the past or the future, but in the present as much as possible. It is a state of inner peace and knowing that no matter what happens everything will work out.

My shoplifting was an outward insane expression of my inner insanity and angry, fearful, twisted thinking. *For a long time, I viewed life as insane and rationalized that stealing was the only sane thing for me in an insane world.* Most addicts believe their addiction is a logical and sane response to life.

In time I became more spiritual and now can access a Higher Power. To do this, I stop or slow down and breathe. I ask myself the right questions or allow myself to be guided by the Higher Power within myself, the Higher wisdom.

Step Three

Made a decision to turn our will and our lives over to the care of our Higher Power as we understood this.

It's one thing to admit you've got a problem and that your life has become a wreck, it's another to admit that you need help and, in a moment of faith, believe that something better is possible for you. But it's a quantum leap to turn your will over, the way you've always known.

Even today, I feel Step Three is the hardest step for me. I see how it's so easy to go in and out of taking my will back. For me, Step Three means not only resisting my will or desire to take shortcuts in life by shoplifting or stealing but actually surrendering my attachment to how I think life should go. After all, this was what really got my stealing going to begin with: the feelings of unfairness that came with life not going how I wanted it to go. Almost every day I am faced with that issue head on. Some days I feel I've been able to let go but I'm still working on it and always will.

When faced with the temptation to shoplift, the "lower power" in us would have us believe there is no other way to ease the pain, that we are entitled to steal, that not to steal is actually a defeat rather than a victory. My will is the part of me that speaks first and speaks loudest. When asked what I want, this part of me says: "I want that thing. I want to hurt someone. I want to get even. I deserve this!" My Higher will responds, when I surrender, to what I *really* want: peace, love, cooperation, to know everything will be okay.

Step Three asks us to turn our lives over to the care of our Higher Power. You've probably said "I've trusted before and look what happened? My way may not be the best way but if it doesn't turn out, at least I can blame myself."

Step Three is a leap of faith. It's no wonder most people, especially addicts, have trouble letting go of their own way and being open to a way from without. When I have mastered this for moments at a time, things usually turn out better than if I had tried to manipulate or handle it myself. For example: My stealing was an effort to make life fair, to get one up on life, but as much as I tried to do this I kept feeling one down. It was insanity, like a mouse going back to the cheese which is no longer there, doing the same thing over and over again and expecting a different result. I could have kept fighting but gradually I realized there had to be another way. I had to let go of my way of going it alone and expecting things to improve. I wouldn't have been able to complete this book if I kept trying to do it myself. My Higher Power guided me to the help of others and to surrendering my battle against life.

Step Four

Make a searching and fearless moral inventory of ourselves.

Step Four has been challenging because it called me to stop blaming the world and look at myself. That was hard to do at first and remains hard when I fall back into feeling like a victim. I essentially began Step Four with my therapist in 1990 when I realized I had to look within, not only at my shoplifting but my stealing and other behaviors I felt guilty about: my mistreatment of my younger brother, my cheating on my girlfriend, my impatience, my greed, my controlling nature. I had to own my shadow side, the things that I didn't want to claim, the aspects of myself I projected onto others, especially onto my father.

In working Step Four I also needed to *recover* the positive aspects of myself, the moral parts of myself which, due to my shame, I had lost touch with. That's where I think the word "recovery" really comes from. I had to reclaim the parts of me that cared about others, that cared about myself, the honest and good parts which were pure and not just for show. In some ways, it was harder for me to reclaim the positive aspects of myself than to acknowledge the negative ones.

Admitted to our Higher Power, to ourselves, and to at least one other human being, the exact nature of our wrongs.

Prior to starting C.A.S.A., I confided in my therapist about the exact nature of my wrongs. This meant getting specific about what I had stolen and how much and from whom, including individuals. It was not enough to just admit that I stole. Some slight catharsis comes with that but nothing lasting.

Further, the exact nature of my wrongs included not only my behavior of stealing but other behaviors. For example, the infidelity, the judging of others, the misuse of my authority. Beneath all the behaviors, the exact nature of my wrongs seemed to be that I was selfish, greedy, controlling, impatient, hypocritical, manipulative, among other qualities. To simplify, I acted mostly out of fear rather than love. I chose fear rather than love and trust. And I had to forgive myself for this. I did the best I could at the time.

Step Five asks we admit this to three sources: Higher Power, ourselves, and another human being. There's the old saying, if you can't be honest with anybody else, at least be honest with yourself. But sometimes it's hard to be honest with yourself unless you make the effort to share with someone else. It is then you remember and realize things you've either forgotten or didn't feel the full impact of. I've found the same thing to be true when opening up a dialogue of prayer, confession, or seeking of forgiveness from my source of Higher Power. I've done this in my mind, out loud, at a place of worship, at my father's grave, writing in a journal. There are many ways to do this. Each should find his or her own way and should not fear experimenting and finding what's best.

In a sense, I've told the world about my shoplifting through this book and through interviews in magazines, newspapers, on the radio and TV. Be careful who you choose to tell. True, it's a risk because you can't know how one will react. But a good start is to pick an impartial, nonjudgmental person such as a minister, rabbi, therapist, sponsor, or trusted friend. Maybe at a confidential support group meeting. Be on guard. Don't use Step Five as a confessional to dump your sins and guilt so you can continue your addiction. I've seen this happen in our support group and I've been guilty of it as well.

Step Six

Were entirely ready to have our Higher Power remove our defects of character.

Step Six is like Step Three for me. Being ready to do anything is scary for most and to open yourself up for real and deep change can feel like facing death, surrendering to death, leaping off a cliff into the great abyss.

What are meant by defects of character? This is tricky. I see these as any parts of myself which lead me or others to suffer. This can be impatience, perfectionism, greed, dishonesty, selfishness, etc. Step Six, like all the steps, is part of an ongoing renewal cycle. It is meant to be repeated over and over again. So don't feel afraid "you have to get it right" the first time. That is perfectionism. Move into Step Six when you have worked through the first five. Enter with a spirit of sincerity and purity in the moment. Meditate on it and open to the inner wisdom and power of it. Be curious. You don't have to have your character defect list in front of you. You know what your defects are; they don't make you a bad person but they keep you from experiencing deeper serenity and growth. Just be open.

An officer recently invited me to observe a two hour intervention he conducts with teen shoplifters. He created this list of common reasons why people shoplift as related to the Seven Deadly Sins: Greed, Envy, Jealousy, Wrath, Sloth, Gluttony, and Lust. Can you relate to any of these?

Step Seven

Humbly asked our Higher Power to remove our shortcomings.

I want to emphasize the word "humbly" because it reminds us that we can't do it ourselves, we don't make demands on Higher Power. We ask and we are patient. The addict puts his faith outside himself to provide a quick fix, whether that faith is in drugs, gambling, or shoplifting. Recovery wisdom recognizes each Step is an ongoing process. So, you need to humbly ask sometimes--or many times--for your shortcomings to be removed as you become more and more ready. Over time, you will gain increasing clarity as to what your shortcomings are. A character defect may be my impatience. My shortcoming may be my impatience with my wife when she takes more time to do something than I would. My perfectionism may be a character defect. My shortcoming may be how I criticize someone when they don't do something up to my standards.

Step Eight

Made a list of all persons we have harmed and became willing to make amends to all.

Through my recovery, I saw I hurt many through my shoplifting addiction; not just as a direct result of my stealing but also as a result of the lies, the betrayal of trust, the inability to love others more fully or to let their love in. The hurt stemmed from the worry they had for me, the built-up anger and bitterness which leaked out onto others in a myriad of ways. My secret, addictive life deprived them of the person they thought they were in relationship with.

Also on my list of those I harmed are the stores from which I shoplifted. While I don't know the people personally, I spent time imagining the harm done to them. It's probably hard for most shoplifting addicts to feel this because the store is impersonal and we don't see directly the hurt our shoplifting causes. It's easy to slip back into feeling like we, ourselves, have been the real victims. But include them in your list. Make a list of any individuals you've stolen from, any jobs, any offices, any parties or other places.

Step Nine

Made direct amends wherever possible except when to do so would injure people.

Making direct amends is an ongoing process. Amends may begin with an apology but then usually requires more. I always say: *The best amend you can give to your friends, family and society is developing a good recovery program and ceasing to engage in destructive behavior.* That's what is asked of us. To make amends for lost trust takes time and patience. Respecting people and property each day is a great way to give back to others. *I started a support group for shoplifting addicts, in part, as a way to give back to society for what I had stolen.*

As for actually returning stolen objects to people or stores, think about that first. Sometimes it can do more harm than good to others and to yourself. Ask yourself: What is my intention in returning an object? Is it to make myself feel better or will it serve others? Sometimes, you'd like to give back what you've taken but you don't feel you can risk it.

Maybe the store people won't be forgiving, maybe they'll prosecute you which can hurt you and your loved ones. What if you returned the object anonymously or made a donation to the store or the person you've stolen from? Maybe you stole a pack of cigarettes from a friend and without telling, bought him another pack. This may or may not be enough. You decide. You have choices.

Step Ten

Continue to take personal inventory and when we are wrong promptly admit it.

This step is very important. Recovery is a process of unraveling and letting go of the past. But, in the meantime, we are living in the present, creating new conflict (or karma) each day, each moment. If we clean up after ourselves as we go along, we create less of a past mess to clean up later. But keep it simple. One of the biggest gifts I've gotten out of my recovery is the ease to admit when I'm wrong. Saying "I was wrong," "You're right," or "I'm sorry," are some of the most liberating words you can speak. A good time to take a personal inventory is at the end of the day or in a support group setting.

Step Eleven

Sought through prayer and meditation to improve our conscious contact with our Higher Power as we understood this, praying only for knowledge of our Higher Power's will for us and the power to carry out that will

Some people ask "why pray or meditate? I'm not stealing anymore, my life is manageable again." I've been there. I'm still there. It's a question of what works and realizing the fullest value of recovery. Remember, addicts are good at fooling themselves into thinking they have control again, that they were the sole cause of the problem and the sole solution. This may seem like an empowering belief. It is not. It is dangerous. I know I played a major role in how I got addicted to shoplifting but I am also a product of my genetics, my family, my environment, my culture, my world. I am susceptible to playing out the unhealthy scripts of the collective consciousness. I need help beyond myself to be myself. Einstein said, "The problems of the world cannot be solved at the level of thinking when the problems were created."

There are many forms of prayer and meditation. For me, each is a way of helping me feel connected to the whole, of centering me, of bringing forth my most authentic and powerful self. Without meditation, I've found again and again, my ego runs rampant and, even if I'm not stealing, I remain miserable and tense. The promise of recovery holds much more than this.

Step Twelve

Having had a spiritual awakening as a result of these steps, we will try to carry this message to other addicts and practice these principles in all our affairs.

In some ways I leaped right to Step Twelve by starting C.A.S.A. before I worked through the other Steps in any thorough way. But I also needed the group to help me realize the Steps. Step Twelve is not an end but a beginning. It is the logical turnaround before returning to Step One. "You only keep what you give away" is a common recovery saying. If I truly have achieved some level of spiritual awakening through my recovery, why would I want to keep it to myself? I'm not saying, go out on the street corner and start preaching and recruiting, but carry your recovery as a gift to share with others who may show up in your life--whether at a meeting table as a newcomer or in your daily affairs. As a recovering caretaker, it becomes dangerously tempting to try to save others again when I am the primary one I need to save. There's a balance. We shall find that balance one day, each day, readjusting from moment to moment. One day at a time.

Notes and Reflections on the 12 Steps:

Life Happens: A Quiz

How would you react to the following life happenings?

*You lose your wallet
*Someone bumps into your car
*You lose your job
*You become ill
*You are lonely
*Someone you know gets all the luck
*The store won't exchange your merchandise
*You are treated rudely by a shopkeeper
*You lose a lot of money in the stock market
*You get a speeding ticket or a flat tire

What life events would trigger you to have an urge to shoplift?

Part Four

Related Topics

Paul M.'s Story

Paul is the manager and co-owner of a Midwest independent retail store. He is soft-spoken and sweet but noticeably hardened and bitter. His short story illustrates how real people are adversely affected by shoplifting and employee theft. Regardless of the type or size of the store, the stress on working people is palpable. There are no nameless, faceless entities involved to steal from, only real people with real lives.

My father started this business in the 1950's and I've been in it about twenty years now. I'm finding it harder and harder to stay in business and I know I'm not the only one. First, it's getting harder and harder for the little guy, the small businesses, to survive in the world of big businesses, franchises, and conglomerates. That's tough enough. But the other challenge in any business, and this is certainly true with ours, is shrinkage, or loss of product by theft.

It's gotten worse and worse over the years. It's both external loss, which is the shoplifting, but more demoralizing is the internal loss, the employee theft. I was reading a retailer statistic the other day and it stated that both forms of theft have gone up in the last two years since 9/11 with the souring economy, but I think the figure for internal loss was the most dramatic, something like 60% increase. I wouldn't doubt it because we've seen so much of it in our business. It's tough. You don't know who you can trust anymore. We've hired friends and family members and even they have stolen. You can't trust anybody anymore. It's sad.

I think it's some kind of entitlement thing with most people, particularly the younger ones who are the people we're most likely to employ. The feeling they have is that stealing's not really wrong, like everybody does it. Sometimes they act on their own but often they do it together. Shoplifting is less of a concern for us than the employee theft.

I don't think they get how much it hurts our family, not just financially but emotionally. I mean, some of these kids we watched grow up. We've mentored them, or at least tried to; some of them we've lent money to, helped them out in other ways, we even sent one of them to college. It's heartbreaking. There's hardly a day I don't dread going into work. I'm always on edge, it's bad enough just trying to run a business but to always have to watch our own workers. It's not fun. They just act like they like you and are loyal to you. We treat our employees well. We like to think, as a small business, that it's more laid back and more personal, a better place to work, but I guess that doesn't matter. We've got employee discounts, rewards, we give them store credit, gift certificates, bonuses, everything to deter them from stealing. Nothing seems to work.

We've discovered so many different schemes, it's amazing. We don't have the best security but we've got some. We do modest background checks, we don't have electronic tags or gates, we do have some security cameras but those are mainly to watch the employees. We don't, however, monitor the cameras as much as we need to, that would be expensive. We have a multi-story building and we've had to close a few of the upper floors. We just use them for storage. The co-workers were dropping stuff out of the windows to each other.

They'd get cell phone calls while on duty or make calls and I know that some of them use them to make calls to each other or to the outside when it's safe to steal, like when I'm busy with a customer. It's crazy. I've tried to ban cell phones from

171

the workplace but there was a big protest. Kids these days feel they need their phones for emergencies or just because it's a basic right. I tried telling them I survived without a phone. If they need to be contacted in case of an emergency, someone can call the store phone. The problem I have, which puts me in a bind, is that it's actually hard to find employees to begin with. If I ban the phones or enforce other strict rules, I may not get anyone to work for me.

As it is, I've had to drastically downsize the business, partly because of the competition and the economy but also, it seems, the more employees I have, the more shrinkage I have. It gets too hard to keep track of 15 employees. Now I'm down to about five. I've considered hiring security guards, installing more sophisticated security systems, doing all kinds of things that the big boys do with their stores. But frankly, they spend millions of dollars and I know they still have problems.

It seems the best employees are the ones who steal the most. They learn the system and do great in sales and customer services, they win your trust and appreciation and then they start turning on you. I've had to let so many of those go. It's almost as if it's better to hire incompetent people because they seem to be less devious.

We have kids who steal from us and have the nerve to wear the clothing to work. It's hard to prove, though. Sometimes they rip the labels off the clothes but that doesn't really do anything except make you more convinced they stole it. And shoes, they have a thing about shoes. It's gotten to the point where I have to ask them what size shoes they wear to keep track of what's missing and who likely stole them.

Besides wearing the clothes they steal or using the other stuff, I know for a fact that a lot of kids are selling things they steal. Once, a customer came back to the store to return something but I ran it through the scanner and there was no record of it being sold. An employee was at the counter and got nervous and tried to take care of it for the customer. That's when I knew. I fired him on the spot. But it's rare that you catch someone red-handed.

A few other times were like when a friend of mine saw an employee selling our items at a local park. I was out of town and, supposedly the employee was off sick that day. I had another incident where I was renting out a house of mine to a few long-term employees. I went to the house one day to check on something and found bags full of stuff they'd stolen from the store. I ended up taking the bags and putting the things back on the shelf at the store the next day. It was quite a scene watching them squirm at work that day. They left my house that day and I knew they weren't coming back to work or to my house. The problem was, I'm sure there were others at work who were in on it, too, but I couldn't prove it.

Imagine going to work each day and feeling like your employees or co-workers are your enemies. It's awful. I experienced intense depression and anxiety. I had other things going on in my life, too. My mother was dying, my marriage was in trouble. People don't stop to think how their actions are affecting others.

I had to let go one of my best employees a while ago. He'd been with us for a long time. I didn't catch him red-handed but I know he was stealing. He still comes in every now and then to say hello and I can tell by his questions that he's still trying to figure out why I let him go. It's killing him. It's torture. I just told him at the time that it was time for him to grow up and move on, there were better things in store for him.

The reason I don't prosecute is that it would take so much time and energy I don't figure it's worth it. Maybe I should. As for the shoplifting, I don't think my employees think it's really wrong. They seem to have a big problem even staying close to the customers, they feel they're smothering them or that the customers will get upset. I tell them, there's an art to it. We're not a self-serve store. Customers are not supposed to go through the store and try everything on and make a mess of the whole store. That's not good business. It takes two hours for an employee to straighten up after them instead of assisting them. Sure, it's also a deterrent to have an employee nearby as well.

Every now and then we'll bring in a consultant or a detective to hang out for a bit and that puts them on edge. But as far as drug testing or other screening, it's hard and expensive to do. I honestly worry that we wouldn't find anyone to work if we asked everybody if they'd ever stolen something small from work. I bet almost everybody would flunk that question, especially if we had a polygraph. It's sad.

Employee Theft

Question: In the workplace, what constitutes stealing?

*Fudging your time card?

*Padding your expense account (if you have one)?

*Making personal phone calls?

*Using company postage?

*Using office supplies for personal use?

*Taking office items home?

*"Borrowing" funds for personal use?

*Making personal copies on the copier?

*Not reporting accounting errors in your favor?

*Taking the company car on personal errands

Is there an issue about asking permission?

Employee theft is a huge problem. It can become addictive. The classic story is the person fired from his or her job for embezzling a half million dollars. We scratch our heads, wondering: "What were they thinking? They didn't actually think they could get away with that?" The answer usually is: "They weren't thinking. They got hooked." It happens a little at a time. Someone's vulnerable--there's a financial or emotional stressor, a conflict at work--and a line is crossed. Next thing you know, your star employee is being hauled away in handcuffs.

Estimates suggest employee theft takes a bigger bite out of stores' profits than shoplifting and, ultimately, adds many other costs to peoples' lives. People may have different ideas of what constitutes employee theft. There is a continuum, degrees of it. But stealing is stealing.

When I got serious about recovery and stopping shoplifting, I realized I couldn't blatantly steal money and goods from

175

the workplace. I knew I was holding onto employee theft in an addictive manner. I still got a bit of a rush from it. I still used it to make myself feel better. I still felt the guilt and shame the addict feels which, ironically, contributes to the behavior continuing. I stole to drown out, if temporarily, the guilt and shame created by the shoplifting. It was unnerving to feel like I'd been caught stealing anytime the boss said he or she wanted to talk to me. It interfered with my work relationships and my ability to do my job my best.

Probation Officer/Counselor Checklist
for Appropriate Referrals to C.A.S.A.

Note: *These are preliminary assessment questions to help guide you. Please use all necessary means of gathering information.*

Questions:	Appropriate	Not Appropriate
1. Are you remorseful about having stolen?	"Yes/Sort of"	"No/Not really"
2. Previous record of shoplifting?	"Yes" *Explore*	"No"
3. Have you suffered a recent loss in your life?	"Yes/Sort of"	"No/Not Really"
4. Are you depressed?	"Yes/Sort of"	"No/Not really"
5. Are you angry/upset about anything in your life?	"Yes/Sort of"	"No/Not really"
6. Do you feel guilty or ashamed of your stealing?	"Yes/Sort of"	"No"
7. Do you steal from other people besides stores	"No/Rarely"	"Yes/ Often"
8. Have you told others about your shoplifting?	"No/Rarely" *Explore*	*Explore*

Questions:	Appropriate	Not Appropriate
9. Do you sell any of the items you shoplift/steal?	"No/Rarely"	"Yes"
10. Have you tried to stop stealing but been unable to?	"Yes/Sort of"	"No/Not really"
11. Do you know why you shoplift/steal?	"No/Sort of"	"Greed/Need"
12. Do you want to stop? If so, why?	"Yes"	"No/Not really"
13. Do you shoplift to sell things to get drugs, alcohol or for gambling?	"No"	"Yes"
14. Do you shoplift/steal due to lack of money?	"No/Not really"	"Yes"
15. Do you shoplift alone?	"Yes"	"No"
Totals:	_____ /	_____

Note: *If the interviewee has identified with most of the questions in the "Appropriate" column, he or she is a good candidate for C.A.S.A. If he or she has identified more with the questions in the "Inappropriate" column, consider treatment, counseling, AA/NA/GA, or other forms of punishment first. Some persons are never appropriate for C.A.S.A.*

Other Questions for Shoplifters

1. Why did you commit this act? (Explore grief, anger, anxiety)

2. When is the first time you stole/shoplifted something?

3. What was going on in your life at the time?

4. How long have you been stealing/shoplifting?

5. Do you commit any other acts of dishonesty?

6. Are you currently in counseling or on medication?

7. Have you previously been in counseling or on medication?

8. Are you under financial stress?

9. Do you have other addictions (alcohol, drugs, gambling)?

10. Do you feel you steal/shoplift due to emotional stress?

11. Do you feel you are addicted to shoplifting/stealing?

12. Would you consider seeing a counselor and/or attending a local support group for people who shoplift/steal?

13. Does anybody else know about your shoplifting/stealing?

14. Do you feel ashamed of your shoplifting/stealing?

15. Have you tried to stop before?

How to Conduct an Intervention

I've had the opportunity to work with many family members and friends of addicts who've struggled with how to confront and support their loved ones. For family or friends of shoplifters or people who steal, this is especially challenging because there is such shame and misunderstanding about these behaviors and few resources to direct them to for help. It's tempting to shout: "Hey, you thief, cut it out! Don't you know that's wrong?" This approach, or similar ones, will push the person farther away from opening up, getting help, and stopping the behavior.

I've talked to parents of children who steal and to many adults whose parents addressed their stealing. *Two approaches don't work:* saying or doing nothing, which sends an unspoken message it is not a big deal; or shaming, yelling, condemning, which sends the indirect message "you are bad" and pushes a child into shutting down his or her feelings. Children steal for various reasons–to get attention, to get a need met, or to test the bounds of their own power and authority.

If you suspect or catch your child stealing, this is an opportunity to talk to them and teach them. I recommend telling them you are concerned about their behavior. Tell them stealing is wrong and explain it in a way children can understand. Don't tell them it's wrong because it's breaking a commandment or they will go to hell. Tell them it's wrong because people are entitled to trust their things will be safe, we need to be honest to feel good about ourselves and to be trusted by others, and we wouldn't like it if our things were taken.

If your child has stolen from a store, a friend, a class mate, encourage him or her to return the item(s) with an apology. In some case, it may be best to go with your child to make sure this happens and assist in the amend or arrange it in advance.

If you feel a consequence or punishment is in order, I recommend it be proportionate to the offense or deferred until the next time it happens. I suggest generous amounts of praise as a better way to mold a child's behavior, especially when he or she has been honest. You don't have to give lavish rewards for honesty because honesty brings its own rewards.

Most people are unaware for a long period of time a loved one has a problem with shoplifting or stealing until you find some clue(s) about it. You may feel awkward about how or if to approach the person. The "evidence" often is circumstantial and you may hesitate to accuse someone. After all, what if you are wrong?

If you are reading this book, you have the advantage of knowledge and sensitivity about the dynamics and reasons people shoplift or steal. Remember, it's an unconscious cry for help. It's easy to be mad at someone but he or she is in pain. You also have the advantage of pointing a person who needs help in the right direction: to this book, our web site, support groups, or the various resources listed at the back of this book.

As Vernon Johnson, author of Intervention, defines it:

"Intervention is a process by which the harmful, progressive, and destructive effects of (an addiction) are interrupted and the (addict) is helped to stop (the addiction) and to develop new and healthier ways of coping with his or her needs or problems. (Or more simply) presenting reality to a person out of touch with it in a receivable way."

You need supportive people at an intervention who have observed firsthand any of the stealing behaviors, the circumstantial clues of the behavior, or any other problems

181

associated with the suspected or known behavior (mood wings, evasiveness, change of lifestyle or interests). If you are the only one who can be involved in the intervention, so be it, but I would suggest you invite at least one trusted mutual friend, minister, counselor or family member to sit in.

Here is an example of how an intervention should go and often does go. You've noticed your spouse has been increasingly evasive or moody. You've found, while cleaning, a variety of objects in the home which you don't remember seeing before. You suspect your spouse may have a problem with shoplifting or stealing because your gut tells you something is fishy, there's been a past history of this behavior, or a family member or friend tells you something is missing from their home or office; you may or may not have found the object in your home. You may not have the "smoking gun" which proves your spouse is stealing but you don't want to wait for that. There's too much at stake–an arrest, a broken relationship, a firing from a job, further loss of trust, a delay in receiving help.

"Dan" has arranged a time at home to get his wife "Lori's" undivided attention. He invited his wife's sister, "Susan," over because she also has suspected her shoplifting.

Dan: "Honey, I'm glad you're here. Susan and I have something important to talk to you about and all we ask is that you listen. We'll give you a chance to talk when we're done. We need you to listen because we care about you."

Lori: (defensive) "What's this about?"

Dan: "We're here because we care about you. We're here to talk about shoplifting. We're not accusing you but we believe you are shoplifting and we have reasons to believe this. We need you to listen to what we need to say."

Lori: "Shoplifting? What are you talking about?"

Dan: "We understand you feel shocked. But we need you to listen to our concerns. For the last two years we've noticed something different about you. You've spent more time away from the home. You've been less social. I thought it was just a phase you were going through."

Lori: "What does this have to do with anything?"

Dan: "Let me finish. I was cleaning the house last week and I found a pile of clothes in the back closet which looked like they've never been worn. I've never seen you in them. I've also seen you with some new jewelry over the last year and I've also noticed over the last two years since Erin went away to college that you quit the gym. I know we've been on a tighter budget since then but you haven't reduced your lifestyle at all. I'm not criticizing, I'm concerned. I went over our credit card bills the other day and it doesn't look like you've used those much. So I don't know where you got those clothes or the jewelry."

Lori: "What are you snooping around for? I have to show you every receipt? I have my own money you know! I don't need to account for everything I bring in the house."

Dan: "Then please explain to me what those new clothes were doing in the back of the closet."

Lori: "They didn't fit--I didn't like them after I bought them. I needed some room in my clothes closet."

Dan: "Why didn't you just take them back to the store?"

Lori: (beginning to get nervous) "I don't know. Why do I have to explain this to you? And what does this have to do with you, Susan?"

Susan: "Because I care about you and I know there's

something wrong. Something's going on with you. I'm not sure if it's stealing or what. If it is, please just tell us. We're not going to yell at you are lecture you. We want to help. We did some research and found out a lot of people steal or shoplift when they have issues. You've been through a lot lately, the changes."

Lori: "You always were the know-it-all, weren't you? Why are you meddling in this anyway?"

Susan: "Lori, we want to help you. You need to trust us. This secret you've been keeping has got to be eating you up inside. We promise. We just want to see you get some help. I miss the old Lori. We're not going to tell anybody else what's going on if that's what you're worried about. But we need you to tell the truth here and agree to get some help or there will be consequences."

Lori: (angrily but fearfully) "Consequences? Like what?"

Dan: "There's already been consequences. A loss of trust. Lori, if you don't get honest here, I don't think our marriage can survive. I don't think you can survive. If you don't get help, I will. I'll go to a counselor myself and find out what I need to do. In the meantime, if you are shoplifting, eventually you're going to get arrested. I don't want to be the one to have to bail you out."

Lori:(sarcastically) "You don't have to worry about me."

Dan: (getting frustrated) This is a sickness. I need you to tell me the truth.

Susan: "Lori, I need to be able to trust you, too. I need to feel comfortable about having you over our house."

Lori: "I've never stolen anything from your house! (beginning to break down) "All I've ever done is give to all of you. I've given my life for you. Nobody appreciates what I've had to sacrifice."

It is best to let the person vent for a bit if they need to.

Lori: (on the verge of tears) "I feel so much pressure. I don't know how to handle it. I'm always last. I don't ask for anything. I have needs, too. I don't know what's happened to me. I'm losing control. I don't know what to do."

Dan: (resisting the urge to save her) "It's okay, honey. That's why we're here. I'd be happy to see what we can do together to work on things. But I need to know: Are you shoplifting?"

Lori: (after a long pause and a deep inhale) "Yes."

The intervention process is a starting point. Once the person admits a problem, you must be firm with consequences and to keep the person on track toward finding outside help. Share options with your loved one and offer reasonable assistance. If the intervention does not work, you may need to try again or make some hard choices to take care of yourself.

There is a theory that there are five stages of change:
1) pre-contemplation
2) contemplation
3) investigation
4) implementation
5) maintenance

Where does your loved one fall in this model? How about you?

Starting a Self-Help Group

I was fortunate by the time I started C.A.S.A. in late 1992 to have already curtailed my shoplifting through counseling and attendance at S.O.S. for a year and a half. I witnessed the support group process and had become able to make a commitment and offer support to others. I had the added support of a two month personal growth seminar which supported my creating C.A.S.A. in my community.

I would have done some things differently but I urge you to be persistent. I showed up 14 consecutive Wednesday evenings before the first person came to our group. Getting media coverage was a big challenge. I secured the place and time of the meetings at the church where my other support group met. I suggest a public place like a church or an activities center. It may be a little awkward asking if a shoplifters group can meet there but you can show them this book or some other literature to prove that it is a legitimate disorder people need help for. That is more than I had to go on.

I mailed out about 50 flyers to the local courts, a few big churches and a few counseling agencies. I did not want my name or phone number on the flyers because I was very concerned and still somewhat ashamed about this. I suggest that you be willing to take a risk to use your phone number, at least, as a contact.

I had a reporter show up at the very first scheduled meeting. I tried to convince the reporter that there were many people who needed help out there but I needed her to help me get the word out. That story never got printed but a few months later I got a hold of another reporter who decided to write an article about our group, me in particular, and how shoplifting increases during the holiday season. This is always an attractive tie-in subject for the media.

Here are some ideas I've used to help start, maintain C.A.S.A.:

1. Establish a meeting place and time
2. Create flyers and mail, post and fax about town especially to courts, churches, counseling offices, newspapers, criminal defense attorneys, bookstores, coffee shops
3. Contact the media (TV, radio, newspapers, magazines)
4. Create a website
5. Post flyers at other support group meetings
6. List your group information with your state self-help clearinghouse which is usually located in your state's capital
7. Write an article (even anonymously) for a paper
8. Notify stores who may pass on the word
9. Ask for ideas or help from friends/family
10. List in your local newspaper's health calendar

List some of your ideas:

1.

2.

3.

4.

5.

6.

7.

8.

9.

10.

Epilogue

Where do we go from here?

In the eleven years since I started C.A.S.A. and embarked upon this personal and professional journey, I have grown in knowledge, compassion, and strength. I have been blessed to have created and been given numerous opportunities to share my story of struggle and success. At times it has been a lonely journey; at others, exhilarating. I have done what I can, as a recovering shoplifter, to reach out to others and help them in various ways: I started C.A.S.A., I've represented shoplifters as an attorney, I've counseled them as a therapist, I started a web site, e-mail support group and chat room, I've held seminars, I've spoken at the courts, I've been on local and national radio and television, and wrote or was featured in numerous articles in magazines and newspapers. Writing this book is my way of getting the word out to more people, to push this issue "over the hump."

I know I will always need help. I pray there are others ready to start groups. I pray there are other professionals seeking education on how to best treat addictive-compulsive shoplifting and theft. I pray people in general open their minds and their hearts to those who suffer from these afflictions. I hope this book proves recovery is possible and paves a way there.

We need more research and study on shoplifting as more than just a legal issue. We need more understanding, more compassion, more treatment options.

As I continue my recovery, I don't know what's next in the design plan for me or for this "movement." I do know I am here to enjoy life.

Resources

*Terrence Shulman, Therapist, Attorney, Consultant & Lecturer
PO Box 250008 Franklin, MI 48025
Phone/Fax 248-358-8508
E-mail: info@shopliftersanonymous.com
Web site: www.shopliftersanonymous.com

*Cleptomaniacs And Shoplifters Anonymous, Detroit, MI
PO Box 250008 Franklin, MI 48025
(248) 358-8508

*Shoplifters Anonymous Manhattan, NY
Attention: Leo R.
PO Box 55 NY, NY 10276
(212) 673-0392

*Shoplifters Anonymous Minneapolis, MN
Attention: Lois L.
PO Box 24515 Minneapolis, MN 55424
(612) 925-4860

*Shoplifters Anonymous San Francisco, CA
Attention: Ed H.
PO Box 316 Petaluma, CA 94953-0316

*Shoplifters Recovery Program San Francisco, CA
Web site: www.shopliftersrecoveryprogram.com
Attention: Elizabeth Corsale
Phone: 415-267-6916

*Dorothy Hickey, Former Probation Officer, London, Ontario
Author of Shoplifting: A Cry for Help, 1996
601-180 Cherryhill Circle London, Ontario, N6H 2M2

*Wil Cupchik, PhD Toronto, Ontario, Canada
Author of Why Honest People Shoplift or Commit Other Acts of Theft, 1997
Web site: www.whyhonestpeoplesteal.com
Phone: 416-928-2262

*Marcus Goldman, MD Boston, MA
Author of Kleptomania, 1997

*John E. Grant, JD, MD and S.W. Kim, MD
Authors of Stop Me Because I Can't Stop Myself: *Taking Control of Impulsive Behavior*, 2002

*Shoplifters Alternative, New Jericho, NY
380 N. Broadway New Jericho, NY 11753
Attention: Peter Berlin
800-848-9595
Web site: www.shopliftersalternative.org

*Theft Talk Counseling Services, Inc., Portland Oregon
3530 S.E. 2nd Street Portland, OR 97206
Web site: www.thefttalk.com
800-88-THEFT (888-4338)

*Shoplifters Anonymous, Palatine, IL
(847) 934-3994